RICHARD EVANS' QUOTE BOOK

by

Richard L. Evans

**Selected from
the "Spoken Word"
and
"Thought for the Day"**

**and from many inspiring
thought-provoking sources
from many centuries**

PUBLISHERS PRESS
Salt Lake City, Utah

RICHARD EVANS' QUOTE BOOK

Copyright © 1971 Atesons

Printed in the United States of America

All rights reserved

For information address Publishers Press

1900 West 2300 South, Salt Lake City, Utah 84119

6th Printing, 1975

LITHOGRAPHED IN U.S.A. BY

PUBLISHERS PRESS
SALT LAKE CITY, UTAH

Contents

EDITOR'S NOTE

For many years I have admired the work of Richard L. Evans — his calm, reassuring radio voice, his unfailing good taste, his far-ranging mind, his sensitivity to language and values, and his spiritual and moral leadership, touching millions of people, worldwide. And so I was honored when asked if I would assist in selecting, organizing, and editing this book of quotations.

Richard L. Evans has, for more than forty years, been the producer, the writer, and the voice of "Music and the Spoken Word" on the Tabernacle Choir broadcast heard on CBS each week from Temple Square in Salt Lake City. This book is the product of a lifetime of his wide-ranging reading and collecting of stimulating thoughts out of the millions of quotable things written and spoken by many people through many centuries, all over the world. During many of those years he has been assisted in this by a discerning secretary, Geniel Robbins, whose invaluable service is gratefully acknowledged. The counsel and assistance of Doyle Green concerning this collection is also acknowledged. Many others have made contributions also. Some excerpts from Richard L. Evans' own writings were suggested and selected by the Editor and others.

This volume is intended not as a typical collection of poetry or prose, but rather as a book of ideas — a book for browsing — not in any particular order — not always literary — sometimes provocative — sometimes whimsical, and yet profound in affirmation of the lasting values of life.

I hope readers will find this collection as stimulating and challenging as I have done, while helping to select and organize it.

Dr. Bruce B. Clark

During the last few days while final copy for publication of the volume was being prepared, Richard L. Evans died, unexpectedly, at the age of 65, on the morning of November 1, 1971. Prior to his death he spent many hours over a period of weeks examining and approving the quotations, and making certain changes and additions, so that the volume stands in a unique way as his final contribution to the world. He was a truly remarkable man, with a great and gentle soul, but also with rich wisdom and humor, and this book is a lasting reflection of his life and values to be treasured by all who admired him and loved him.

B.B.C.

Part 1

Home, Marriage, Mothers, Fathers, Families

The kindest and the happiest pair,
Will find occasion to forbear;
Find something every day they live,
To pity, and perhaps forgive.

—WILLIAM COWPER

NO other success can compensate for failure in the home.

—*David O. McKay*

WHERE does the family start? It starts with a young man falling in love with a girl.

—*Sir Winston Churchill*

DO not think you can make a girl lovely if you do not make her happy.

—*John Ruskin*

WINNING a love once is not enough. Keep *rewinning* it. . . . In the last analysis, it's up to you to save your marriage.

—*Hubert S. Howe*

THE most important thing a father can do for his children is to love their mother.

—*Author Unknown*

MARRY . . . into a family that will enable your children to feel proud of both sides of the house.

—*Robert E. Lee*

THE sum which two married people owe to one another defies calculation. It is an infinite debt, which can only be discharged through all eternity.

—*Johann Wolfgang von Goethe*

IT comes as a great surprise to younger people that a husband and wife must work at marriage *all* the years of their life.

—*Dr. May E. Markewich*

THE trouble with being a parent is that by the time you are experienced you are usually unemployed.

—*Author Unknown*

DO you expect, forsooth, that a mother will hand down to her children principles which differ from her own?

—*Juvenal*

HE shall turn the heart of the fathers to the children, and the heart of the children to their fathers.

—*Old Testament, Malachi 4:6*

BE ever gentle with the children God has given you. Watch over them constantly; reprove them earnestly, but not in anger.

—*Elihu Burritt*

IF we had paid no more attention to our plants than we have to our children, we would now be living in a jungle of weeds.

—*Luther Burbank*

A woman can stand anything but being forgotten, not being needed.

—*Mary Stewart Cutting*

A happy family is but an earlier heaven.

—*Sir John Bowring*

MARRIAGE: The best method ever devised for becoming acquainted.

—*Arnold Glasow*

IT is not good that man should be alone.

—*Old Testament, Genesis 2:18*

NEITHER is the man without the woman, neither the woman without the man, in the Lord.

—*New Testament, I Corinthians 11:11*

FOR this cause shall a man leave his father and mother, and cleave to his wife; And they twain shall be one flesh: . . . What therefore God hath joined together, let not man put asunder.

—*New Testament, Mark 10:6-9*

THE memory of a mother waiting is a safeguard against temptation.

—*Author Unknown*

I remember my mother's prayers and they have always followed me. They have clung to me all my life.

—*Abraham Lincoln*

I have observed all day your patience with baby, your obedience and kindness to all. Go on trying, my child. God will give you strength and courage. I shall say a little prayer over you in your sleep. Mother.

—*Mother of Louisa May Alcott*

WHERE'S Mother," could be heard through the hallway. And they stood and watched her as she went on alone, and the gates closed after her. And they said: "We cannot see her, but she is with us still. A mother like ours is more than a memory. She is a Living Presence."

—*Temple Bailey*

TO bear, to nurse, to rear,
To watch and then to lose,
To see my bright ones disappear,
Drawn up like morning dews.

—*Jean Ingelow*

YOU may have tangible wealth untold;
Caskets of jewels and coffers of gold.
Richer than I you can never be—
I had a mother who read to me.

—*Strickland Gillilan*

HER heart was the abode of heavenly purity. She had no feelings but of kindness and beneficence. . . . She had known sorrow, but her sorrow was silent. . . . If there is existence and retribution beyond the grave, my mother is happy.

—*John Quincy Adams*

SONGS my mother taught me,
In the days long vanish'd
Seldom from her eyelids
Were the teardrops banish'd.
Now I teach my children
Each melodious measure,
Oft the teardrops flowing,
Oft they flow from my mem'ry's treasure.

—*Author Unknown*

THE sweetest sounds to mortals given
Are heard in Mother, Home and Heaven.

—*William Goldsmith Brown*

IT is sobering when a father sees in his son himself, his mannerisms, his ways, his words. It is a great moment in life when a father sees a son grow taller than he, or reach farther. It is a blessed thing for fathers to see their sons exceed them.

—*Richard L. Evans*

ONE father is worth more than a hundred school masters.

—*George Herbert*

COMPANIONED years have made them comprehend
The comradeship that lies beyond a kiss.
The young ask much of life — they ask but this,
To fare the road together to its end.

—*Roselle Mercier Montgomery*

BACKWARD, turn backward, O Time, in your flight,
    Make me a child again just for tonight!
Mother, come back from the echoless shore,
    Take me again to your heart, as of yore;
Kiss from my forehead the furrows of care,
    Smooth the few silver threads out of my hair;
Over my slumbers your loving watch keep,
    Rock me to sleep, Mother, rock me to sleep.

—Elizabeth Akers Allen

FAITH that withstood the shocks of toil and time;
    Hope that defied despair;
    Patience that conquered care;
And loyalty, whose courage was sublime;
The great deep heart that was a home for all,—
    Just, eloquent, and strong
    In protest against wrong;
Wide charity, that knew no sin, no fall;
The Spartan spirit that made life so grand,
    Mating poor daily needs
    With high, heroic deeds,
That wrested happiness from Fate's hard hands.

—Louisa May Alcott

A father will do well, as his son grows up . . . to talk familiarly
with him; . . . The sooner you treat him as a man, the sooner
he will begin to be one: and if you admit him into serious dis-
courses . . . with you, you will . . . raise his mind above the
usual amusements of youth, and those trifling occupations which
it is commonly wasted in. . . . Nothing cements and establishes
friendship and good-will so much as confident communication. . . .
When your son sees you open your mind to him [he will know
he has] a friend and . . . father.

—John Locke

THE bravest battle that ever was fought;
　　Shall I tell you where and when,
On the maps of the world you will find it not;
　　It was fought by the mothers of men.

Nay, not with cannon or battle shot,
　　With sword or braver pen;
Nay, not with eloquent word or thought,
　　From the mouths of wonderful men.

But deep in a woman's walled-up heart—
　　Of woman that would not yield,
But patiently, silently bore her part—
　　Lo! there in that battlefield.

No marshaling troop, no bivouac song;
　　No banners to gleam and wave;
And oh! these battles they last so long—
　　From babyhood to the grave!

Yet, faithful still as a bridge of stars,
　　She fights in her walled-up town—
Fights on and on in the endless wars,
　　Then silent, unseen—goes down.

　　　　　　　　　　—Joaquin Miller

THERE are some wonderful words in our language, words that are inseparably associated: home, mother, father, family — and in our thoughts they are linked in fondest and most meaningful remembrance.

Where the normal pattern prevails, father is more away and less closely acquainted with the daily problems and program. But fathers are people in whose footsteps sons are apt to follow, and with whose hearts daughters are likely to have their way.

Fathers are people by whose name the family is known. Fathers are people whom sons and daughters should feel free to approach with their problems. There are hazards in going it alone in life, and fathers are to talk to — even if they seem to be too busy; even if they are doing so much for the family in other ways that they are not enough at home.

　　　　　　　　　　—Richard L. Evans

ALL things need watching, working at, caring for, and marriage is no exception. Marriage is not something to be indifferently treated or abused, or something that simply takes care of itself. Nothing neglected will remain as it was or is, or will fail to deteriorate. All things need attention, care and concern, and especially so in this most sensitive of all relationships of life.

—*Richard L. Evans*

PARENTS have a duty to govern their children. But the object of all good government is to prepare the subject for self-government.

—*Dr. Lyman Abbott*

WHAT gift has Providence bestowed on man that is so dear to him as his children?

—*Cicero*

TWO persons who have chosen each other out of all the [rest], with the design to be each other's mutual comfort and entertainment, have, in that action, bound themselves to be good-humored, affable, discreet, forgiving, patient, and joyful, with respect to each other's frailties and perfections, to the end of their lives.

—*Joseph Addison*

THIS is the true nature of home — it is the place of Peace; the shelter, not only from all injury, but from all terror, doubt, and division.

—*John Ruskin*

I desire no future that will break the ties of the past.

—*George Eliot*

CHILDREN do not know how their parents love them, and they never will till the grave closes over those parents, or till they have children of their own.

—*Edmund Vance Cooke*

TIS sweet to know there is an eye will mark our coming, and look brighter when we come.

—*Lord Byron*

THE most important work you will do for the Church will be within the walls of your own home.

—*Harold B. Lee*

ASK yourselves whether your household is kept open by pure, refined, unselfish, elevated living. . . . In the home, hearts ought to lie nearest and openest to one another.

—*Phillips Brooks*

FATHERS, provoke not your children to wrath: but bring them up in the nurture and admonition of the Lord.

—*New Testament, Ephesians 6:4*

THE first duty to children is to make them happy.—If you have not made them so, you have wronged them. —No other good they may get can make up for that.

—*Charles Buxton*

I have commanded you to bring up your children in light and truth.

—*Doctrine & Covenants 93:40*

THE mother in her office holds the key of the soul; and she it is who stamps the coin of character.

—*Author Unknown*

THEY shall also teach their children to pray, and to walk uprightly before the Lord.

—*Doctrine & Covenants 68:28*

MAN scans with scrupulous care the character and pedigree of his horses, cattle and dogs before he matches them: but when he comes to his own marriage he rarely, or never, takes any such care.

—*Charles Darwin*

HAPPY will that house be in which the relationships are formed from character.

—*Ralph Waldo Emerson*

CHILDREN, obey your parents in all things: for this is well pleasing unto the Lord.

—*New Testament, Colossians 3:20*

THE idea that we can leave entirely to children the vital choices of life is unsafe. Leaving such decisions to trial and error is unsafe.

—*Richard L. Evans*

TRAIN up a child in the way he should go: and when he is old, he will not depart from it.

—*Old Testament, Proverbs 22:6*

IT is not marriage that fails, it is people that fail. All that marriage does is to show people up.

—*Harry Emerson Fosdick*

MARRIAGE should be something worked toward with every step you take. It shouldn't be an unforeseen emergency, like being called upon unexpectedly to make a speech on a subject you've never heard of.

—*Margaret Lee Runbeck*

MARRIAGE is a fine and sacred thing if you make it so.

—*William Lyon Phelps*

NOW sharper than a serpent's tooth it is to have a thankless child!

—*Shakespeare*

HE is the happiest, be he king or peasant, who finds peace in his home.

—*Johann Wolfgang von Goethe*

THE best thing to spend on children is your time.

—*Arnold Glasow*

WHEN one puts business or pleasure above his home, he that moment starts on the downgrade to soul-weakness.

—*David O. McKay*

AN infallible way to make your child miserable is to satisfy all his demands.

—*Henry Home*

WHAT greater ornament . . . to a father than a son's honorable conduct?

—*Sophocles*

THE happiest moments of my life have been the few which I have passed at home in the bosom of my family.

—*Thomas Jefferson*

ABSTRACTED from home, I know no happiness in this world.

—*Thomas Jefferson*

CHILDREN have more need of models than of critics.

—*Joseph Joubert*

THE most vicious enemy to home life is immorality.

—*David O. McKay*

THE deepest tenderness a woman can show to a man is to help him do his duty.

—*Dinah Maria Mulock*

THE future destiny of the child is always the work of the mother.

—*Napoleon Bonaparte*

NOT my will, nor even thy will; but *our* will, subject always to His will.

—*Author Unknown*

KEEP thy eyes wide open before marriage; and half shut afterward.

—*Thomas Fuller*

IF thou wouldst be happy and easie in thy Family, above all things observe Discipline. Every one in it should know their Duty. . . . And whatever else is done or omitted, be sure to begin and end with God.

—*William Penn*

FOR a wife take the daughter of a good mother.

—*Thomas Fuller*

THE home where happiness securely dwells
Was never wrought by charms or magic spells
A mother made it beautiful, but knew
No magic save what toiling hands can do.

—*Arthur Wallace Peach*

TAKE a child by the hand and you take a parent by the heart.

—*Author Unknown*

MARRIAGE requires the giving and keeping of confidences, the sharing of thoughts and feelings, unfailing respect and understanding, and a frank and gentle communication.

—*Richard L. Evans*

THE best goal is the success of the marriage itself.

—*Dr. Paul W. Popenoe*

A grateful son, long happily married, told in one short sentence what his father had said when he confided in his father concerning his coming marriage to a lovely girl. This his father said: *"Be good to her — and treat her like a queen."*

—*Thomas S. Priday*

DO they miss me at home—do they miss me?
'Twould be an assurance most dear,
To know that this moment some loved one
Were saying, "I wish he were here."

—*Caroline Atherton Briggs Mason*

CHILDREN are travellers newly arrived in a strange country of which they know nothing.

—*John Locke*

IN general those parents have the most reverence who deserve it.

—*Samuel Johnson*

WHATEVER woman may cast her lot with mine, should any ever do so, it is my intention to do all in my power to make her happy and contented; and there is nothing I can imagine that would make me more unhappy than to fail in the effort.

—*Abraham Lincoln*

A certain woman was heard to say as she observed a manly young man: "I would give twenty years of my life to have such a son." And the mother of the young man was heard to say: "That's what I *have* given — twenty years of my life to have such a son."

—*Author Unknown*

THE art of living together happily is perhaps one of the greatest of all the arts . . . Naturally, . . . all sorts of adjustments are called for. . . . Quarrels and disputes are sure to come, [but] the great thing is not to let them *last*.

—*William Lyon Phelps*

LET thy child's first lesson be obedience.

—*Benjamin Franklin*

I would have them desire and claim the title of Lady, provided they claim, not merely the title, but the office and duty signified by it. . . . Queens you must always be; . . . queens to your husbands and your sons; queens . . . to the world beyond, which bows itself . . . [to] the stainless scepter of womanhood.

—*John Ruskin*

WHAT a father says to his children is not heard by the world, but it will be heard by posterity.

—*Jean Paul Richter*

CHILDREN have a right to be protected from exploitation and from evil influence.

—*Richard L. Evans*

HE that flies from his own family has far to travel.

—*Gauis Petronius*

IF I were asked to name the world's greatest need, I should say unhesitatingly; wise mothers and . . . exemplary fathers.

—*David O. McKay*

THE Crown of the house is Godliness.
The Beauty of the house is Order.
The Glory of the house is Hospitality.
The Blessing of the house is Contentment.

—*Old Inscription*

I have spread my dreams under your feet;
Tread softly because you tread on my dreams.

—*William Butler Yeats*

INSTEAD of saying to a bride, "Hold your husband," . . . we should say, "Love your husband."

—*Margaret W. Jackson*

MARRIAGE is for adults only" — not necessarily of years, but maturity of attitude — the maturity to know that there aren't any perfect people, that nothing is ever altogether as anticipated, that the years change us and others. Marriage requires the maturity to adjust, to forgive, to understand, to be forgiven.

—*Richard L. Evans*

SEEK always to please each other, but in doing so keep heaven in mind.

—*Frederika Bremer*

THE courage or sincerity [of girls is hardly] thought of half so much importance as their way of coming in at a door; . . . [We bring] for the purpose of our own pride, the full glow of the world's worst vanity upon a girl's eyes, at the very period when the whole happiness of her future . . . depends upon her remaining undazzled.

—*John Ruskin*

TAKE not too short a time to make a world-without-end bargain in.

—*Shakespeare*

BACK of every achievement is a proud wife and a surprised mother-in-law.

—*Brooks Hays*

THE home is the source of our national life," said David O. McKay. It is also the source of our personal lives, and in a sense the determiner of our everlasting lives. And so our plea is for parents to take the time it takes to draw near to the children God has given them. Let there be love at home. Let there be tenderness and teaching and caring for and not a shifting of responsibility onto others. God grant that we may never be too busy to do the things that matter most, for "Home makes the man!"

—*Richard L. Evans*

A CHILD learns more by imitation than in any other way. Don't we all? And the persons he imitates most blindly and trustingly are bound to be his parents. . . . Nature has made the relationship between parent and child such that beside it any other training bears a certain artificiality.

—*George Sanderlin*

IT is a common saying that "Manners make the man;" and there is a second, that "Mind makes the man;" but truer than either is a third, that "Home makes the man." For the home-training includes not only manners and mind, but character. It is mainly in the home that the heart is opened, the habits are formed, the intellect is awakened, and character is molded for good or for evil.

—*Samuel Smiles*

HEARKEN unto thy father that begat thee, and despise not thy mother when she is old.

—*Old Testament, Proverbs 23:22*

IF you were paddling a canoe together, the important thing is that each paddle in the same direction. In marriage, if each has a different goal, they will always be in trouble.

—*Dr. Paul W. Popenoe*

HE that has . . . no such connecting interests . . . as a home and a family . . . is exposed to temptation, to idleness, and in danger of becoming useless, if not a burden and a nuisance in society.

—*Samuel Johnson*

PEACE and rest at length have
    come,
All the day's long toil is past;
And each heart is whispering, 'Home,
    Home at last!'

—*Thomas Hood*

MY FATHER transmitted to me a sound heredity on his own side, and gave me a good mother.

—*Alice Stone Blackwell*

ONE of my students wrote me announcing his engagement. "This is not going to be much of a wedding," he said, "but it is going to be a wonderful marriage."

—*William Lyon Phelps*

A great proportion of the wretchedness which has embittered married life, has originated in a negligence of trifles. . . . It is a sensitive plant, which will not bear even the touch of unkindness; a delicate flower, which indifference will chill and suspicion blast. It must be watered by the showers of tender affection, expanded by the cheering glow of kindness, and guarded by the impregnable barrier of unshaken confidence. Thus matured, it will bloom with fragrance in every season of life, and sweeten even the loneliness of declining years.

—*Thomas Sprat*

WITH death, marriage is one of life's two greatest adventures. . . . I would keep it an adventure — an adventure in happiness.

—*Frances Starr*

SO much of what is great . . . has sprung from the closeness of the family ties.

—*Sir James M. Barrie*

THE best cure for restlessness for far places is to go there and find them full of people who would like to get back home again.

—*Anne Sophie Swetchine*

AN ideal wife is any woman who has an ideal husband.

—*Booth Tarkington*

ONE reason for a child's walking in wrong ways would be in his not knowing which way to walk. One reason for his going his own way would be if his parents did not unitedly know which way they want him to go. Agreement between parents on fundamentals, basic beliefs, is among the foremost essentials for a solid family, for the solid teaching of children. And in this there must be sincerity, because children will surely detect the signs of insincerity in any partnership of parents. They will feel the tensions and the differences even when they can't say why they are so.

Division between parents is unfair and confusing and weakens the foundations of the family. Those to whom a child should most look for guidance, must be united in the guidance they give. Blessed are those whose parents have achieved a partnership, a solid working of a team of two.

—Richard L. Evans

THE education of a child begins in infancy. At six months old it can answer smile by smile, and impatience with impatience. It can observe, enjoy, and suffer. Do you suppose it makes no difference to it that the order of the house is perfect and quiet, the faces of its father and mother full of peace, their soft voices familiar to its ear, and even those of strangers, loving; or that it is tossed from arm to arm, [in a] . . . reckless . . . household, or in the confusion of a gay one? The moral disposition is, I doubt not, greatly determined in those first speechless years.

—John Ruskin

WOULD you have your son obedient to you when past a child; be sure then to . . . imprint it in his infancy; . . . so shall you have him . . . obedient . . . whilst he is a child, and your affectionate friend when he is a man. . . . For the time must come, when [he] will be past the rod and correction; . . . and he that is a good, a virtuous, and able man, must be made so within. And therefore what he is to receive from education, what is to sway and influence his life, must be something . . . woven into the very principles of his nature . . . The little, or almost insensible impressions on our tender infancies, have very important and lasting consequences.

—John Locke

INFANCY isn't what it is cracked up to be. Children, not knowing that they are having an easy time, have a good many hard times. Growing and learning and obeying rules of their elders, or fighting against them, are not easy things to do.

—*Don Marquis*

I think we are inclined to forget that youth and beauty are [after] all . . . only lures. They are not binders . . . We stress too much the externals and forget too much the realities . . . There are greater hazards to marriage than attraction for other people.

—*Margaret W. Jackson*

A young man was once asked . . . why he did not . . . marry a certain very beautiful but rather frivolous girl. . . . "Is she a person whom you would pick out to entrust with the bringing up of your children?" he said. When his questioners conceded this was not so, he added, "Well, I do not choose to entrust her with the bringing up of mine."

—*Alice Stone Blackwell*

YOU see that boy of mine? Though but five, he governs the universe. Yes, for he rules his mother, his mother rules me, I rule Athens, and Athens the world.

—*Themistocles*

THERE is little less trouble in governing a private family than a whole kingdom.

—*Montaigne*

GOD has given us no greater blessing than that of belonging to a loving and loyal family — and it will be so, always and forever.

—*Richard L. Evans*

A truly happy marriage is one in which a woman gives the best years of her life to the man who made them the best.

—*Author Unknown*

MEN should not suffer reverses and unpleasant circumstances to sour their natures and render them fretful and unsocial at home, speaking words full of bitterness . . . to their wives and children, creating gloom and sorrow in their habitations, making themselves feared rather than beloved by their families.

—*Brigham Young*

SWEET is the smile of home; the mutual look when hearts are of each other sure.

—*John Keble*

FOR a couple who have basked in the sunshine of each other's love to stand by and see the clouds of misunderstanding and discord obscure the lovelight of their lives is tragedy indeed.

—*David O. McKay*

TO be happy at home is the ultimate result of all ambition.

—*Samuel Johnson*

WE have been so anxious to give our children what we didn't have that we have neglected to give them what we *did* have.

—*Author Unknown*

THE parents that you should honor more than any others are the parents of your children-to-be. Those children are entitled to the best parents that it is possible for you to give them — clean parents.

—*N. Eldon Tanner*

A man travels the world over in search of what he needs, and returns home to find it.

—*George Moore*

COURAGE, and be true to one another!

—*Thomas Carlyle*

THERE is beauty all around
    When there's love at home;
There is joy in every sound
    When there's love at home.
Peace and plenty here abide,
Smiling sweet on every side.
Time doth softly, sweetly glide
    When there's love at home.

In the cottage there is joy
    When there's love at home;
Hate and envy ne'er annoy
    When there's love at home.
Roses bloom beneath our feet;
All the earth's a garden sweet,
Making life a bliss complete
    When there's love at home.

Kindly heaven smiles above
    When there's love at home;
All the world is filled with love
    When there's love at home.
Sweeter sings the brooklet by;
Brighter beams the azure sky;
Oh, there's One who smiles on high
    When there's love at home.

—*Author Unknown*

WE are foolish, and without excuse foolish, in speaking of the 'superiority' of one sex to the other, as if they could be compared. ... Each completes the other, and is completed by the other. ... You may chisel a boy into shape, as you would a rock, or hammer him into it, if he be of a better kind, as you would a piece of bronze. But you cannot hammer a girl into anything. She grows as a flower does ... you cannot fetter her; she must take her own fair form and way, and have — "Her household motions light and free, And steps of virgin liberty."

—*John Ruskin*

LATELY I have thought a lot about 'listening,' " said Hannie Struve. "How often you hear a little child complain . . . 'you're not *listening!*' And how easily the mother replies, 'What do you *want?*' And mostly the child does not really 'want' anything, only to communicate."

Take time to listen — to children, young people, others! Sometimes they are reluctant to seek counsel because they receive impatient replies.

"Why do we parents so often say, 'I'm busy now,' " asked Robert M. Neal. "Why do we . . . not realize that a child is like a sunbeam, here for a moment and then gone somewhere else."

Talking — listening — patience, willingness to learn enough before jumping to quick conclusions: Sometimes in just letting them talk and using us for listening, they will come soberly, safely to their own conclusions. But when two people both talk at once, when they cut each other short, or when they don't talk at all, there aren't likely to be any satisfactory solutions.

Yes, it takes time to listen, but it takes more time to correct mistakes once they have been made. With too many misjudging, too many making mistakes, with too few taking time to listen, counsel cannot seem as satisfactory as it should.

"The key is communication," reported a *Time* essay. " 'Can't you see I'm busy?' . . . ought to be banned. 'Listen' ought to be [implanted] over every parent's heart."

If only we could feel we have been heard! If only we would listen when we should!

—*Richard L. Evans*

DEAR Lord, make me a better parent. Teach me to understand my children, to listen patiently to what they have to say and to answer all their questions kindly. Keep me from interrupting them, talking back to them, and contradicting them. Make me as courteous to them as I would have them to be to me.

—*Gary Cleveland Myers*

Dear Dad,

I am writing this to you, though you have been dead thirty years. . . .

I feel I must say some things to you, things I didn't know when I was a boy in your house. . . .

It's only now, after passing through the long hard school years, only now, when my own hair is gray, that I understand how you felt.

I must have been a . . . trial to you. . . . I believed my own petty wisdom. . . .

Most of all, I want to confess my worst sin against you. It was the feeling I had that you 'did not understand.'

When I look back over it now, I know that you did understand. You understood me better than I did myself. . . .

And how patient you were with me! How full of long-suffering, and kindness!

And how pathetic, it now comes home to me, were your efforts to get close to me. . . .

What was it held me aloof? I don't know. But it is tragic — that wall that rises between a boy and his father. . . .

I wish you were here now, across the table from me, just for an hour, so that I could tell you how there's no wall any more; I understand you now, Dad, and, how I love you, and wish I could go back and be your boy again. . . .

Well, it won't be long, Dad, till I am over [there], and I believe you'll be the first one to take me by the hand and help me. . . .

I know that [among] the richest, most priceless things on earth, and the thing least understood, is that mighty love and tenderness and craving to help, which a father feels toward his boy.

For I have a boy of my own. . . .

Up there somewhere in the Silence, hear me, Dad, and believe me.

—Dr. Frank Crane, (Four Minute Essays: Dad)

THE success of children is the success of parents. The sorrow of children is the sorrow of parents.

—*Richard L. Evans*

OUT of the dreariness,
Into its cheeriness,
Come we in weariness
Home

—*Stephen Chalmers*

Part 2

Youth and Age

Young folks ought to know that we old folks know more about being young than they know about being old.

—Author Unknown

I am always interested in how big things begin. You know how it is; you're young, you make some decisions . . . then swish, you're seventy. You've been a lawyer [or something else] for over fifty years and that white-haired lady by your side has eaten over 50,000 meals with you. How do such things begin?

—*Thornton Wilder*

How beautiful is youth! how bright it gleams
With its illusions, aspirations, dreams!
Book of Beginnings, Story without End,
Each maid a heroine, and each man a friend.

—*Henry Wadsworth Longfellow*

GROW old along with me!
    The best is yet to be,
The last of life, for which the first was made:
    Our times are in His hand
    Who saith, "A whole I planned,
Youth shows but half; trust God; see all, nor be afraid!"

—*Robert Browning*

MEN and women are what happened to little boys and girls.

—*Author Unknown*

THE future of the race marches forward on the feet of little children.

—*Phillips Brooks*

IF we could be twice young and twice old, we could correct all our mistakes.

—*Euripides*

TO me, old age is always fifteen years older than I am.

—*Bernard Baruch*

FOR myself, I had rather be an old man a somewhat shorter time than an old man *before* my time.

—*Cicero*

A boy is the only known substance from which a man can be made.

—*Author Unknown*

THE excesses of our youth are drafts upon our old age, payable with interest, about thirty years after date.

—*Charles Caleb Colton*

WITH the ancient is wisdom; And in length of days understanding.

—*Old Testament, Job 12:12*

IT is better to build boys than to repair men.

—*Author Unknown*

I remember my youth and the feeling that I could last forever, outlast the sea, the earth, and all men.

—*Joseph Conrad*

PLEASANT memories are the welcome companions of our aging years.

—*Richard L. Evans*

I used to wonder a little at the serene faith of the old. . . . I wonder no more. I can see that the day is far spent, and I begin to feel that serenity of faith which had excited my wonder. I feel, more and more, like one going home. Going home is a good part of the occupation of every living thing. Home is the polestar of this planet. It is a universal, ever-present force.

—*Irving Bacheller*

YOU'LL find as you grow older that you weren't born such a very great while ago after all.

—*William Dean Howells*

WHEN saving for old age, be sure you put away a few pleasant thoughts.

—*Author Unknown*

THE old have what the young wish they had: The one wishes to live long; the other has lived long.

—*Cicero*

IF youth be a defect, it is one that we outgrow only too soon.

—*James Russell Lowell*

WHATEVER poet, orator, or sage
May say of it, old age is still old age.
It is the waning, not the crescent moon;
The dusk of evening, not the blaze of noon:
It is not strength, but weakness; not desire,
But its surcease; not the fierce heat of fire,
The burning and consuming element,
But that of ashes and of embers spent,
In which some living sparks we still discern,
Enough to warm, but not enough to burn.
What then? Shall we sit idly down and say
The night hath come; it is no longer day?
The night hath not yet come; we are not quite
Cut off from labor by the failing light;
Something remains for us to do or dare;
Even the oldest tree some fruit may bear; . . .
For age is opportunity no less
Than youth itself, though in another dress,
And as the evening twilight fades away
The sky is filled with stars, invisible by day.

—*Henry Wadsworth Longfellow*

THE brain is like a muscle. The more you use it, the more it develops. That's the opinion of leading scientists who studied the relationship of mental ability to aging. In other words, a seventy-five-year-old who has been exercising his brain is more likely to be mentally sharp and alert than a fifty-five-year-old whose brain has been half asleep since he got out of school.

—*Martin E. Segal*

EXCEPT ye . . . become as little children, ye shall not enter into the kingdom of heaven. Whosoever therefore shall humble himself as this little child, the same is greatest in the kingdom of heaven.

—*New Testament, Matthew 18:3-4*

SUFFER the little children to come unto me, and forbid them not: for of such is the kingdom of God.

—*New Testament, Mark 10:14*

CHARACTER is always associated with something old and takes time to grow, like the beautiful facial lines of a man in middle age, lines that are the steady imprint of man's evolving character. . . . We love old cathedrals, old furniture, old silver, old dictionaries and old prints, but we have entirely forgotten about the beauty of old men. I think an appreciation of that kind of beauty is essential to our life.

—*Lin Yutang*

THE unused talent now going to waste among persons who think they are on the shelf could win world peace, mitigate racial tensions, help economically less advanced people . . . and give new hope to life throughout the world.

—*Joy Elmer Morgan*

I have often thought what a melancholy world this would be without children; and what an inhuman world without the aged.

—*Samuel Taylor Coleridge*

OLD persons are creatures of habit. Almost everything is impulse with a little child, and nothing can be called habit; almost everything is habit in . . . old age, and there is very little that can be called impulse. As character to be used for eternity must be formed in time and in good time, so good habits to be used for happiness in this life must be formed early.

—*George B. Cheever*

A person soon learns how little he knows when a child begins to ask questions.

—*Richard L. Evans*

THE soul is healed by being with children.

—*Fyodor Mikhailovich Dostoevsky*

WE should cease fighting age as if it were a foe. Memories of past experience may be even sweeter than these experiences were in reality. . . . When a pleasure is in prospect we are disturbed by the fear it may not be realized. But a pleasure in retrospect is secure.

—*Ralph W. Sockman*

WHO is such a fool as to feel certain — however young he may be — that he will be alive in the evening. Indeed, youth has many more chances of death than old age. Aging is a part of living. Aging slows as we grow older. What is natural must be accounted good. And old age is natural.

—*Cicero*

THE child's grief throbs against its little heart as heavily as the man's sorrow, and the one finds as much delight in his kite or drum, as the other in striking the springs of enterprise, or soaring on the wings of fame.

—*Edwin Hubbet Chapin*

I have endeavored to impress upon the minds of youth the necessity of . . . working to the extent of their ability; and also while so laboring never to become disheartened.

—*Heber J. Grant*

THE principal difference between men and boys is the cost of their toys.

—*Author Unknown*

MEN . . . who have no resources in themselves . . . find every age burdensome. There is a quiet, pure, and cultivated life which produces a calm and gentle old age. The qualities best adapted to [it] are culture and active exercise of the virtues. If they have been maintained at every period . . . the harvest they produce is wonderful.

—*Cicero*

TIME has laid his hand
Upon my heart, gently, not smiting it,
But as a harper lays his open palm
Upon his harp to deaden its vibrations.

—*Henry Wadsworth Longfellow*

THE light cannot come, except through purity and righteousness; lust and iniquity are surely darkness. . . . Oh, that there could thrill through the being of our young men some electrical sense that they are God's sons, that they might . . . live the life and attain the nature which are rightly theirs.

—*Phillips Brooks*

I could not at any age be content to take my place in a corner by the fireside and simply look on. Life was meant to be lived. One must never, for whatever reason, turn one's back on life.

—*Eleanor Roosevelt*

FOOLS impute their . . . frailties and guilt to old age. But the fact is that the blame for all complaints of that kind is to be charged to character, not to a particular time of life: unreason and churlishness cause uneasiness at every time of life.

—*Cicero*

TO youth I have but three words of counsel — Work, work, work.

—*Bismarck*

TO be seventy years young is sometimes far more cheerful and hopeful than to be forty years old.

—*Oliver Wendell Holmes*

AGE is the top of a mountain high;
Rarer the air, and blue.
A long hard climb, a bit of fatigue;
But Oh! What a wonderful view!

—*Author Unknown*

IT is in youth that we plant our chief habits and prejudices; it is in youth that we take our party as to profession, pursuits and matrimony. In youth, therefore, the turn is given; in youth the education even of the next generation is given; in youth the private and public character is determined; and the term of life extending but from youth to age, life ought to begin well from youth, and more especially before we take our party as to our principal objects.

—*Benjamin Franklin*

THE belief that youth is the happiest time of life is founded on a fallacy. The happiest person is the person who thinks the most interesting thoughts. . . . As we advance in years we really grow happier, if we live intelligently. . . . To say that youth is happier than maturity is like saying that the view from the bottom of the tower is better than the view from the top. As we ascend, the range of our view widens immensely; the horizon is pushed farther away. Finally as we reach the summit it is as if we had the world at our feet.

—*William Lyon Phelps*

THEY are idols of hearts and of households;
    They are angels of God in disguise;
The sunlight still sleeps in their tresses,
    His glory still gleams in their eyes;
These truants from home and from Heaven,
    They have made me more manly and mild;
And I know now how Jesus could liken
    The kingdom of God to a child.

—*Charles M. Dickinson*

MOONS waxed and waned, the lilacs bloomed and died,
In the broad river ebbed and flowed the tide,
Ships went to sea, and ships came home from sea,
And the slow years sailed by and ceased to be.

—*Henry Wadsworth Longfellow*

I shall grow old, but never lose life's zest,
Because the road's last turn will be the best.

—*Henry Van Dyke*

NOBODY grows old merely by living a number of years; people grow old by deserting their ideals. Years wrinkle the skin, but giving up enthusiasm wrinkles the soul. Worry, doubt, self-distrust, fear, and despair — these are the long years that bow the head and turn the growing spirit back to dust. You are as young as your faith, and as old as your doubts; as young as your self-confidence, as old as your fears; as young as your hope, as old as your despair.

—*Zoroaster*

LET me grow lovely, growing old—
So many fine things do;
Laces, and ivory, and gold,
And silks need not be new.

And there is healing in old trees,
Old streets a glamour hold;
Why may not I, as well as these,
Grow lovely, growing old?

—*Karle Wilson Baker*

A little more tired at close of day,
A little less anxious to have our way;
A little less ready to scold and blame,
A little more care of a brother's name;
And so we are nearing our journey's end,
Where time and eternity meet and blend.

—*Rollin John Wells*

DON'T wait to be a great man — be a great boy.

—*Author Unknown*

YOU can take no credit for beauty at sixteen. But if you are beautiful at sixty, it will be your own soul's doing.

—*Marie Carmichael Stopes*

A good man dies when a boy goes wrong.

—*Author Unknown*

THERE is an old man up there ahead of you that you ought to know. . . . Whether he is miserable or happy, depends on you. For *you* made him. He is *you*, grown older.

—*Author Unknown*

LORD, thou knowest better than I myself that I am growing older and will some day be old. Keep me from the fatal habit of thinking I must say something on every subject and on every occasion. Release me from craving to straighten out everybody's affairs. Make me thoughtful but not moody; helpful but not bossy. With my vast store of wisdom, it seems a pity not to use it all, but Thou knowest, Lord, that I want a few friends at the end.

Keep my mind free from the recital of endless details; give me wings to get to the point. Seal my lips on my aches and pains. They are increasing and love of rehearsing them is becoming sweeter as the years go by. I dare not ask for grace enough to enjoy the tales of others' pains, but help me to endure them with patience.

I dare not ask for improved memory, but for a growing humility and lessening cocksureness when my memory seems to clash with the memories of others. Teach me the glorious lesson that occasionally I may be mistaken.

Keep me reasonably sweet; I do not want to be a Saint — some of them are so hard to live with — but a sour old person is one of the crowning works of the devil. Give me the ability to see good things in unexpected places and talents in unexpected people. Give me the grace to tell them so. Amen.

—Author Unknown

THE young, whether they know it or not, live on borrowed property.

—Sir Richard Livingstone

THE harvest of old age is the memory and rich store of blessings laid up in earlier life.

—Cicero

THE tragedy of life is not that it ends so soon, but that we wait so long to begin it.

—Richard L. Evans

OH, it's a long, long while
From May to December,
But the days grow short
When you reach September.
When the autumn weather turns the leaves to flame,
One hasn't got time for the waiting game.

—Maxwell Anderson

GO placidly amid the noise and the haste, and remember what peace there may be in silence. As far as possible, without surrender, be on good terms with all persons. Speak your truth quietly and clearly; and listen to others, even to the dull and the ignorant; they, too, have their story. . . .

Enjoy your achievements as well as your plans. Keep interested in your own career; it is a real possession in the changing fortunes of time. Exercise caution in your business affairs, for the world is full of trickery, but let this not blind you to what virtue there is; many persons strive for high ideals, and everywhere life is full of heroism.

Be yourself. Especially do not feign affection, neither be cynical about love; for in the face of all aridity and disenchantment, it is as perennial as the grass.

Take kindly to the counsel of the years, gracefully surrender the things of youth. Nurture strength of spirit to shield you in sudden misfortune. But do not distress yourself with dark imaginings: many fears are born of fatigue and loneliness.

Beyond a wholesome discipline, be gentle with yourself. You are a child of the universe no less than the trees and the stars; you have a right to be here. And whether or not it is clear to you, no doubt the universe is unfolding as it should. Therefore be at peace with God, . . . and whatever your labors and aspirations, in the noisy confusion of life, keep peace in your soul. With all its sham, drudgery, and broken dreams, it is still a beautiful world.
Lift up your hearts — be not afraid!

—Max Ehrmann

WHEN *is youth? Who is youth?* Youth is a time we move through swiftly. Youth doesn't last very long — no more than any other age — and it should neither be an *over* privileged nor an *under* privileged segment of society — because at some time it is all of us —as other ages are.

And to you who are young: it won't be long before *you* are "older." And those who follow will ask what *you* have done with *your* life, as you ask this now of others.

Remember, time is crowding you, *right now* — pushing you through your teens to your twenties, and then your thirties and forties — and so on — sooner than you suppose. And almost before you know it, *you* will be "those who are older." And how will you look and feel, as *you* reach the other end?

Youth isn't the permanent property of anyone. It is a corridor we pass through, without lingering very long. There is no stopping place for any of us. And all of us, young or old, should respect each other, at all ages — for our strength is not in a society of segments, but in making the most of the whole length of life.

Who is youth? *When* is youth? Well, it isn't a clique or a club in which we can claim perpetual place. It's a time of life we all go through, quite swiftly, quite soon.

Oh, beloved young friends: Remember life is forever — but youth doesn't last very long. Live to make memories that will bless the *whole* length of your life.

—*Richard L. Evans*

I would rather be ashes than dust! I would rather that my spark should burn out in a brilliant blaze than it should be stifled by dryrot. I would rather be a superb meteor, every atom of me in magnificent glow, than a sleepy and permanent planet. The proper function of man is to live, not to exist. *I shall not waste my days in trying to prolong them. I shall use my time.*

—*Jack London*

IS this the little girl I carried,
   Is this the little boy at play?
I don't remember growing older—
   When did they? . . .

Sunrise, Sunset—
   Swiftly fly the years.
One season following another,
   Laden with happiness and tears . . .

—*Sheldon Harnick*

Part 3

Work, Idleness, Duty, and Doing

The way to be nothing is to do nothing.

—NATHANIEL HOWE

MEN do less than they ought, unless they do all that they can.

—*Thomas Carlyle*

THANK God every morning when you get up that you have something to do that day which must be done whether you like it or not.

—*Charles Kingsley*

THE outlook for our country lies in the quality of its idleness.

—*Irwin Edman*

FOR I am haunted night and day
By all the deeds I have not done.
O unattempted loveliness!
O costly valor never won!

—*Marguerite Wilkinson*

HARD work never killed a man but it sure has scared a lot of them.

—*Author Unknown*

NO one should retire from work. If he does, he will shrivel up into a nuisance — talking to everybody about pains and pills and income tax. When I'm not working, I get tired of myself.

—*Herbert Hoover*

I never did a day's work in my life — it was all fun.

—*Thomas A. Edison*

IT is no use saying "We are doing our best." You have got to succeed in doing what is necessary.

—*Sir Winston Churchill*

ABSENCE of occupation is not rest; A mind quite vacant is a mind distressed.

—*William Cowper*

IN the sweat of thy face shalt thou eat bread.

—*Old Testament, Genesis 3:19*

I believe that we are here to work, and I believe that there is no escape from it. I think that we cannot get into our brain that desire too soon. Work we must if we shall succeed or if we shall advance. There is no other way.

—*J. Rueben Clark, Jr.*

IN idleness there is perpetual despair.

—*Thomas Carlyle*

WE have too many people who live without working, and we have altogether too many who work without living.

—*Charles R. Brown*

GOD sells us all things at the price of labor.

—*Leonardo da Vinci*

IF ever American society and the United States government are demoralized . . . it will come from the voracious desire of office — this struggle to live without toil.

—*Abraham Lincoln*

TO have no regular work, no set sphere of activity, — what a miserable thing it is! . . . To have all . . . wants satisfied is something intolerable — the feeling of stagnation, which comes from pleasures that last too long.

—*Arthur Schopenhauer*

GIVE what you have. To some one, it may be better than you dare to think.

—*Henry Wadsworth Longfellow*

NEVER despair. But if you do, work on in despair.

—*Edmund Burke*

YOU just can't be miserable as long as you are properly and enjoyably busy; there is no room for misery. . . . Work is the best wonder drug ever devised by God.

—*Dr. Orlando Battista*

A man's perfection is his work.

—*Thomas Carlyle*

THERE is no development physically or intellectually without effort, and effort means work.

—*Calvin Coolidge*

THOU shalt not be idle; for he that is idle shall not eat the bread nor wear the garments of the laborer.

—*Doctrine & Covenants 42:42*

IF it isn't worth working at it isn't worth being in.

—*Author Unknown*

LABOR is the divine law of our existence.

—*Giuseppe Mazzini*

THE force, the mass of character, mind, heart or soul that a man can put into any work, is the most important factor in that work.

—*A. P. Peabody*

INACTIVITY, were it only for physiological reasons, is a torment to a healthy human being. . . . Inactivity speedily becomes a torment as soon as the normal craving for rest and leisure has been satisfied.

—*Henri De Man*

ONLY through dedicated work does a man fulfill himself.

—*William S. Carlson*

DO your work; meet life as it is; know that each service is essential — and never be bored.

—*Richard L. Evans*

ONLY a life lived for others is a life worthwhile.

—*Albert Einstein*

OF the thousands of mentally and emotionally abnormal persons I have observed in more than half a century, I believe the one most frequent denominator among them has been a lack of worthy purpose in useful service in society; to make some definite and at least partially unselfish contribution to the world.

—*Dr. James T. Fisher*

LIFE is hardly respectable if it has no generous task, no duties or affections that constitute a necessity of existence.

—*Ralph Waldo Emerson*

MAN must work. That is certain as the sun. But he may work grudgingly or he may work gratefully; he may work as a man, or he may work as a machine. There is no work so rude that he may not exalt it; no work so impassive that he may not breathe a soul into it; no work so dull that he may not enliven it.

—*Henry Giles*

IF you want knowledge, you must toil for it; if food, you must toil for it; and if pleasure, you must toil for it. Toil is the law. Pleasure comes through toil, and not by self-indulgence and indolence. When one gets to love work, his life is a happy one.

—*John Ruskin*

THE greatest use of a life is to spend it on something that outlasts it.

—*William James*

LABOR is one of the great elements of society . . . labor, intelligent, manly, independent, thinking and acting for itself, earning its own wages, . . . educating childhood, maintaining worship, claiming the right of the elective franchise, and helping to uphold the great fabric of the State — that is American labor.

—*Daniel Webster*

IF you will let me, I will wish you in your future what all men desire — enough work to do, and strength enough to do your work.

—*Rudyard Kipling*

FOR great and low there's but one test,
'Tis that each one shall do his best;
Who works with all the strength he can,
Shall never die in debt to man.

—*Author Unknown*

FOR that is the thing a man is born to . . . to expend every particle of strength that God Almighty has given him in doing the work he finds he is fit for; to stand up to it to the last breath of life, and to do his best. We are called upon to do that. . . . I would bid you stand up to your work, whatever it may be, and not be afraid of it.

—*Thomas Carlyle*

THE greater part of human misery is caused by indolence.

—*G. C. Lichtenberg*

I am glad the eight-hour day had not been invented when I was a young man.

—*Thomas A. Edison*

DOING nothing for others is the undoing of ourselves.

—*Horace Mann*

BEHOLD, could ye suppose that ye could sit . . . and because of the exceeding goodness of God ye could do nothing and he would deliver you?

—*Book of Mormon, Alma 60:11*

LET us realize that the privilege to work is a gift, that power to work is a blessing, that love of work is success.

—*David O. McKay*

WORK is not a curse, it is the prerogative of intelligence, the only means to manhood, and the measure of civilization.

—*Calvin Coolidge*

NOTHING will sustain you more potently, than the power to recognize in your humdrum routine, . . . the true poetry of life — the poetry of the commonplace, of the ordinary man, of the plain, toil-worn woman, with their love and their joys, their sorrows and their griefs.

—*Sir William Osler*

IF we don't try we don't do, and if we don't do, what are we on this earth for?

—*From Shenandoah*

NOTHING does itself — that is, nothing constructive. Some-one has to do everything. Lessons don't learn themselves; classes don't teach themselves; food doesn't prepare itself; dishes and other household duties don't do themselves; the very sick don't serve themselves; machines don't make themselves; words don't memorize themselves; skills don't develop themselves; projects don't plan themselves; buildings don't build themselves. Someone has to lay every brick and drive every nail, make everything that is made, do everything that is done, think everything that is thought.

—Richard L. Evans

HE who works with his hands is a laborer;
He who works with his hand and his head is an artisan;
He who works with his hand and his head and his heart is an artist.

—T. V. Smith

REST is not quitting the busy career;
Rest is the fitting of self to one's sphere;
It's loving and serving the highest and best;
It's onward, unswerving; and this is true rest.

—Johann Wolfgang von Goethe

VERY often one must first overcome laziness and lack of inclination. Then there are various impediments. Sometimes victory comes easily, sometimes inspiration entirely escapes me. But I believe it is the duty of an artist never to submit, for laziness is a strong human trait, and nothing is more harmful to an artist than to let laziness get the better of him. One cannot afford to sit and wait for inspiration; she is a guest who does not visit the lazy but comes to those who call her.

—Peter Ilyich Tschaikovsky

THERE is an aura of grandeur about the dull routine of main-tenance. . . . It is easier to build than to maintain. Even a lethargic or debilitated population can be galvanized for awhile to achieve something impressive, but the energy that goes into maintenance of things in good repair day in and day out is the energy of true vigor. . . . It is easier to win our freedom, build a nation and subdue a continent, than it is now to maintain that freedom, and live peaceably with ourselves.

—Eric Hoffer and Clifton G. M. Kerr

DO your duty to the best of your power, win the approbation of your conscience; and popularity, in its best and highest sense, is sure to follow.

—*Sir John Pakington*

ALL higher motives, ideals, conceptions, sentiments in a man are of no account if they do not come forward to strengthen him for the better discharge of the duties which devolve upon him in the ordinary affairs of life.

—*Henry Ward Beecher*

IT is only those who do not know how to work that do not love it. To those who do, it is better than play.

—*J. H. Patterson*

NONE so little enjoy themselves, and are such burdens to themselves, as those who have nothing to do. Only the active have the true relish of life.

—*John Jay*

YOU give but little when you give of your possessions. It is when you give of yourself that you truly give.

—*Kahlil Gibran*

A man is relieved and gay when he has put his heart into his work and done his best; but what he has said or done otherwise shall give him no peace.

—*Ralph Waldo Emerson*

LOVE, therefore, labor; . . . It is wholesome to the body and good for the mind.

—*William Penn*

I never did anything worth doing by accident, nor did any of my inventions come by accident. They came by work.

—*Thomas A. Edison*

IDLENESS alone is without hope: work earnestly at anything, you will by degrees learn to work at almost all things.

—*Thomas Carlyle*

NO man needs sympathy because he has to work. . . . Far and away the best prize that life offers is the chance to work hard at work worth doing.

—*Theodore Roosevelt*

WE are not sent into the world to do anything into which we cannot put our hearts. We have certain work to do for our own bread, and that is to be done strenuously; other work to do for our delight, and that is to be done heartily. Neither is to be done by halves, but with a will, and what is not worth this effort is not to be done at all.

—*John Ruskin*

WHATEVER there is of greatness in the United States, or indeed, in any other country, is due to labor.

—*Ulysses S. Grant*

THE latest Gospel in this world is Know thy work and do it. . . . Blessed is he who has found his work.

—*Thomas Carlyle*

AS steady application to work is the healthiest training for every individual, so is it the best discipline of a state. Honorable industry always travels the same road with enjoyment and duty, and progress is altogether impossible without it.

—*Samuel Smiles*

I don't know what your destiny will be, but one thing I know: the only ones among you who will be really happy are those who have sought and found how to serve.

—*Albert Schweitzer*

THE labor and sweat of our brows is so far from being a curse that without it our very bread would not be so great a blessing. — If it were not for labor, men could neither eat so much, nor relish so pleasantly, nor sleep so soundly, nor be so healthful, so useful, so strong, so patient, so noble, nor so untempted.

—*Jeremy Taylor*

I returned, and saw under the sun, that the race is not to the swift.

—*Old Testament, Ecclesiastes 9:11*

THE greatest asset of any nation is the spirit of its people, and the greatest danger that can menace any nation is the breakdown of that spirit — the will to win and the courage to work.

—*George B. Cortelyou*

WITHOUT labor nothing prospers.

—*Sophocles*

THE man without a purpose is like a ship without a rudder — a waif, a nothing, a no man. Have a purpose in life, and having it, throw such strength of mind and muscle into your work as God has given you.

—*Thomas Carlyle*

THE fruit derived from labor is the sweetest of all pleasures.

—*Vauvenargues*

WORK is as much a necessity to man as eating and sleeping.

—*Karl W. Humboldt*

THE man who does not work for the love of work but only for money is not likely to make money nor to find much fun in life.

—*Charles M. Schwab*

WHAT the world lacks most today is men who occupy themselves with the needs of other men. In this unselfish labor a blessing falls on both the helper and the helped.

—*Albert Schweitzer*

EACH will find that happiness in this world mainly depends on the work he does, and the way in which he does it.

—*Brigham Young*

THERE is a perennial nobleness, and even sacredness, in work. . . . There is always hope in a man who actually and earnestly works.

—*Thomas Carlyle*

IF the devil find a man idle, he'll set him to work.

—*Scottish Proverb*

WHEN ye are in the service of your fellow beings ye are only in the service of your God.

—*Book of Mormon, Mosiah 2:17*

THE highest reward for man's toil is not what he gets for it, but what he becomes by it.

—*Author Unknown*

LABOR is life.

—*Thomas Carlyle*

ALL true Work is sacred; in all true Work, were it but true hand-labor, there is something of divineness. Labor, wide as the Earth, has its summit in Heaven.

—*Thomas Carlyle*

EVERY man's task is his life-preserver.

—*George B. Emerson*

IT is not enough to be industrious; so are the ants. What are you industrious about?

—*Henry David Thoreau*

NOT to be occupied, and not to exist, amount to the same thing.

—*Voltaire*

PRAY for a good harvest, but keep on plowing.

—*Author Unknown*

WORK is a spiritual necessity.

—*Neal A. Maxwell*

WE are all blind until we see
    That in the human plan
Nothing is worth the making, if
    It does not make the man.
Why build these cities glorious
    If man unbuilded goes?
In vain we build the world, unless
    The builder also grows.

—*Edwin Markham*

MAKE the most of yourself, for that is all there is to you.

—*Ralph Waldo Emerson*

YOU have not done enough, you've never done enough, so long as you have something more to contribute.

—*Dag Hammerskjold*

WE can't do everything for everyone everywhere, but we can do something for someone somewhere.

—*Richard L. Evans*

YOU cannot help men permanently by doing for them what they could and should do for themselves.

—*James L. Phillips*

WORK is the grand cure for all the maladies and miseries that ever beset mankind — honest work, which you intend getting done.

—*Thomas Carlyle*

✣♔ Part 4 ♔✣

Success and Failure; Adversity and Opportunity; Decision and Direction

The first thing a fellow ought to do after he learns he's been born equal is to try to outgrow it.

—AUTHOR UNKNOWN

DON'T let life discourage you: Everyone who got where he is had to begin where he was.

—*Richard L. Evans*

A man sits as many risks as he runs.

—*Henry David Thoreau*

THE secret of success in life is for a man to be ready for his opportunity when it comes.

—*Benjamin Disraeli*

WHERE one door shuts another opens.

—*Cervantes*

A wise man will make more opportunities than he finds.

—*Francis Bacon*

RESTLESSNESS is discontent and discontent is the first necessity of progress. Show me a thoroughly satisfied man and I will show you a failure.

—*Thomas A. Edison*

DECIDE what you want to be — pay the price and be what you want to be.

—*John A. Widtsoe*

IT would be an inconvenient rule if nothing could be done until everything can be done.

—*Sir Winston Churchill*

WE are not endeavoring to get ahead of others, but to surpass ourselves.

—*Hugh B. Brown*

IF any of you have a desire to be mediocre, you will probably find that you have already achieved your ambition.

—*Hugh B. Brown*

GOOD luck is another name for tenacity of purpose.

—*Ralph Waldo Emerson*

SOME people want to homogenize society everywhere. I'm against homogenization in art, in politics, in every walk of life. I want the cream to rise.

—*Robert Frost*

AFFLICTION comes to us all, not to make us sad, but sober; not to make us sorry, but wise. . . . It is trial that proves one thing weak and another strong. . . . A cobweb is as good as the mightiest cable when there is no strain upon it.

—*Henry Ward Beecher*

WHAT is it that makes men suppose that they can more easily do twice tomorrow what they didn't do once today!

—*Richard L. Evans*

THE journey of a thousand miles begins with one step.

—*Lao-tse*

YOU see things; and you say "why?"
But I dream things that never were; and I say "why not?"

—*George Bernard Shaw*

WHERE one succeeds because of his smartness, ten succeed because of their faithfulness.

—*Author Unknown*

AH, but a man's reach should exceed his grasp,
Or what's a heaven for?

—*Robert Browning*

THIS one thing I do, forgetting those things which are behind, and reaching forth unto those things which are before, I press toward the mark.

—*New Testament, Philippians 3:13-14*

A life devoted to trifles, not only takes away the inclination, but the capacity for higher pursuits.

—*Hannah More*

WHAT a day may bring a day may take away.

—*Thomas Fuller*

OUR responsibility is not discharged by the announcement of virtuous ends.

—*John F. Kennedy*

GREAT men are said to have four things in common. . . . They speak softly, have the capacity for hard work, a deep conviction for their cause, a consuming belief in their ability to do it.

—*John D. Hess*

THE art of progress is to preserve order amid change and to preserve change amid order.

—*Author Unknown*

THE only purpose of your activity is to get results.

—*Charles C. Johnson*

GOOD is done by degrees.

—*George Crabbe*

MAN, without opposition or competition, would loaf out his life and die a limpid lump of flesh.

—*Author Unknown*

THE power of little things has so often been noted that we accept it as an axiom, and yet fail to see, in each beginning, the possibility of great events.

—*F. P. Edwards*

AFFLICTION is a treasure, and scarce any man hath enough of it. No man hath affliction enough that is not matured and ripened by it and made fit for God.

—*John Donne*

MAN'S actions are the picture book of his creeds.

—*Ralph Waldo Emerson*

PERSISTENT people begin their success where others end in failure.

—*Edward Eggleston*

TAKE all the swift advantage of the hours.

—*Shakespeare*

ONE great artist was asked which of all his productions was the greatest. His prompt answer was: "The next."

—*Author Unknown*

IT'S not what you were, it's what you are today.

—*David Marion*

DO the best you can. That's bad enough.

—*Anthony C. Lund*

LIFE gives to all the choice. You can satisfy yourself with mediocrity if you wish. You can be common, ordinary, dull, colorless, or you can channel your life so that it will be clean, vibrant, progressive, useful, colorful, rich.

—*Spencer W. Kimball*

MOST people are in favor of progress; it's the changes they don't like.

—*Author Unknown*

FROM the earliest years of youth the record does matter very much: the school record, the work record, the moral record, the record of all our conduct and acts and utterances and attitudes. People constantly classify us. Our own acquaintances and companions classify us from the earliest age of remembrance. They know whether or not we are clean and honest or otherwise; willing or lazy; dependable or undependable — and they remember. And those who haven't known us refer to the record when they have reason to, to see if we have the essentials for any trust or office or opportunity.

—*Richard L. Evans*

BEHOLD, I have refined thee . . . ; I have chosen thee in the furnace of affliction.

—*Old Testament, Isaiah 48:10*

THE greatest results in life are usually attained by simple means and the exercise of ordinary qualities. These may for the most part be summed in these two — common sense and perseverance.

—*Owen Feltham*

WHAT a man can imagine or conceive in his mind he can accomplish. Impossibles are possible as thinking men make them so.

—*Henry J. Kaiser*

NEVER leave that till tomorrow which you can do today.

—*Benjamin Franklin*

I hate to see things done by halves. — If it be right, do it boldly, — if it be wrong, leave it undone.

—*Bernard Gilpin*

WHAT on earth would a man do with himself if something did not stand in his way?

—*H. G. Wells*

TO go about your work with pleasure, to greet others with a word of encouragement, to be happy in the present and confident in the future; this is to have achieved some measure of success in living.

—*Edwin Osgood Grover*

THE secret of all success is to know how to deny yourself. . . . Every step of our progress toward success is a sacrifice.

—*Roswell Dwight Hitchcock*

PEOPLE do not lack strength; they lack will.

—*Victor Hugo*

THE future is bought with the present.

—*Samuel Johnson*

MY country owes me no debt. It gave me, as it gives every boy and girl, a chance. It gave me schooling, independence of action, opportunity for service, and honor. In no other land could a boy from a country village, without inheritance or influential friends, look forward with such unbounded hope. My own life has taught me what America means. I am indebted to my country beyond human power to repay.

—Hebert Hoover

ONE of the illusions of life is that the present hour is not the critical decisive hour. Write it on your heart that every day is the best day of the year. He only is right who owns the day, and no one owns the day who allows it to be invaded by worry, fret and anxiety. Finish every day, and be done with it. You have done what you could.

—Ralph Waldo Emerson

FAREWELL! a long farewell to all my greatness!
This is the state of man: today he puts forth
The tender leaves of hope, to-morrow blossoms,
And bears his blushing honors thick upon him;
The third day comes a frost, a killing frost;
And—when he thinks, good easy man, full surely
His greatness is a-ripening—nips his root,
And then he falls, as I do. I have ventur'd,
Like little wanton boys that swim on bladders,
This many summers in a sea of glory,
But far beyond my depth; my high blown pride
At length broke under me, and now has left me,
Weary and old with service, to the mercy
Of a rude stream, that must forever hide me.
Vain pomp and glory of this world, I hate ye!
I feel my heart new-opened. Oh! how wretched
Is that poor man that hangs on princes' favors!
There is, betwixt that smile we would aspire to,
That sweet aspect of princes, and their ruin,
More pangs and fears than wars or women have;
And when he falls, he falls like Lucifer,
Never to hope again.

—John Fletcher from "Henry VIII"
Wolsey's Farewell to his Greatness

FOR it must needs be, that there is an opposition in all things.

—*Book of Mormon, II Nephi 2:11*

AND now, beware of rashness.— Beware of rashness, but with energy, and sleepless vigilance, go forward.

—*Abraham Lincoln*

NO road is too long to the man who advances deliberately and without undue haste; and no honors are too distant for the man who prepares himself for them with patience.

—*Jean de La Bruyere*

THERE is always room at the top, but the elevator is not running. You must walk up the stairs on your own feet.

—*David Starr Jordan*

HISTORY fails to record that any nation has ever shown good prospects of providing abundance and happiness for all, when only a few were doing the thinking, or when only a few were making the decisions.

—*Richard L. Evans*

WITHOUT some goal and some effort to reach it, no man can live.

—*Fyodor Mikhailovich Dostoevsky*

THERE are no times in life when opportunity, the chance to be and do, gathers so richly about the soul as when it has to suffer. Then everything depends on whether the man turns to the lower or the higher helps. If he resorts to mere expedients and tricks, the opportunity is lost. He comes out no richer nor greater; nay, he comes out harder, poorer, smaller for his pain. But, if he turns to God, the hour of suffering is the turning hour of his life.

—*Phillips Brooks*

WE can do anything we want to if we stick to it long enough.

—*Helen Keller*

I cannot give you the formula for success, but I can give you the formula for failure — try to please everybody.

—*Herbert Bayard Swope*

IF I have made any improvement in the sciences, it is owing more to patient attention than anything beside.

—*Sir Isaac Newton*

THERE is no security on this earth; there is only opportunity.

—*Douglas MacArthur*

EVEN genius is but fine observation strengthened by fixity of purpose. Every man who observes vigilantly and resolves steadfastly grows unconsciously.

—Edward G. Bulwer-Lytton

THE trouble with most self-made men is that they stopped too soon.

—Author Unknown

WE must preserve the incentive to succeed and the right to fail.

—Richard L. Evans

MOUNTAINS viewed from a distance seem to be unscalable, but they *can* be climbed, and the way to begin is to take the first upward step. From that moment the mountains are less high. The slopes that seem so steep from a distance seem to level off as we near them.

—Author Unknown

TO be what we are, and to become what we are capable of becoming, is the only end of life.

—Robert Louis Stevenson

NOTHING great was ever achieved without enthusiasm.

—Ralph Waldo Emerson

I hold a doctrine, to which I owe not much, indeed, but all the little I ever had, namely, that with ordinary talent and extraordinary perseverance, all things are attainable.

—Thomas Fowell Buxton

IT is important not to lean on other people because in time you will be unable to do things yourself.

—Dolores Del Rio

HE who is firmly seated in authority soon learns to think security, and not progress, the highest lesson of statecraft.

—James Russell Lowell

HE who is not ready today will be less so tomorrow.

—Ovid

THERE is no point at which having arrived we can remain.

—Author Unknown

SUCCESS or failure depends more upon attitude than upon capacity. . . . Successful men act as though they have accomplished or are enjoying something. Soon it becomes a reality. Act, look, feel successful, conduct yourself accordingly, and you will be amazed at the positive results.

—Dr. DuPree Jordan, Jr.

No one could endure adversity if, while it continued, it kept the same violence that its first blows had. . . . No state is so bitter that a calm mind cannot find in it some consolation. . . . It is possible to soften what is hard . . . and burdens will press less heavily upon those who bear them skillfully.

—*Seneca*

The secret of success is constancy of purpose.

—*Benjamin Disraeli*

I do the very best I know how — the very best I can; and I mean to keep on doing so.

—*Abraham Lincoln*

If to do were as easy as to know what were good to do. . . .

—*Shakespeare*

The darkest day in life is the one in which we expect something for nothing.

—*Allen Shawn*

Come, my friends,
'Tis not too late to seek a newer world.

—*Alfred Lord Tennyson*

A ship in harbor is safe, but that is not what ships are built for.

—*John A. Shedd*

A second rate Something is better than a first rate Nothing.

—*Author Unknown*

One of the marks of the executive is the ability to decide. One of the obligations of free men is the willingness to decide. One of the qualities of effective people is the courage to decide.

—*Richard L. Evans*

I know of no more encouraging fact than the unquestionable ability of man to elevate his life by a conscious endeavor.

—*Henry David Thoreau*

Beautiful thoughts hardly bring us to God until they are acted upon. No one can have a true idea of right until he does it.

—*William R. Inge*

Life is thickly sown with thorns, and I know no other remedy than to pass quickly through them. The longer we dwell on our misfortunes, the greater is their power to harm us.

—*Voltaire*

If you chase two rabbits, both will escape.

—*Author Unknown*

A successful man cannot realize how hard an unsuccessful man finds life.

—*E. W. Howe*

SOME men have thousands of reasons why they cannot do what they want to, when all they need is one reason why they can.

—*Dr. Willis R. Whitney*

THERE are no limitations to what you can do, except the limitations of your own mind as to what you cannot do. Don't think you cannot; think you can.

—*Author Unknown*

AND again, I would that ye should learn that he only is saved who endureth unto the end.

—*Doctrine & Covenants 53:7*

SOMETIMES suddenly, if we haven't done so sooner, we come to realize that just going to be going, just talking to be talking, just spending to be spending, just rushing to be rushing, doesn't really mean much. And periodically we need to appraise our past performance, to repent and improve, and to resolve to follow through the good things we undertake to do.

—*Richard L. Evans*

THE best preparation for the future is the present well seen to, and the last duty done.

—*George Macdonald*

I am at war 'twixt will and will not.

—*Shakespeare*

THE dogmas of the quiet past are inadequate to the stormy present. The occasion is piled high with difficulty, and we must arise with the occasion. As our case is new, so we must think anew and act anew.

—*Abraham Lincoln*

WHEN we're through changing — we're through!

—*Paul H. Dunn*

A fool beholdeth only the beginning of his works, but a wise man taketh heed to the end.

—*Author Unknown*

BEGIN at home.
Be successful and solvent in your own business and professions.
Serve your communities — your church — your country — and many good causes.
Reach out worldwide, and do something for someone, somewhere.

—*Richard L. Evans*

ADVERSITY has ever been considered the state in which a man most easily becomes acquainted with himself.

—*Samuel Johnson*

SEEK not for fresher founts afar, Just drop your bucket where you are.

—*Sam Walter Foss*

COME, come ye Saints, no toil nor labor fear;
  But with joy wend your way.
Though hard to you this journey may appear,
  Grace shall be as your day.
'Tis better far for us to strive
Our useless cares from us to drive;
Do this, and joy your hearts will swell —
All is well! all is well!

Why should we mourn or think our lot is hard?
  'Tis not so; all is right.
Why should we think to earn a great reward,
  If we now shun the fight?
Gird up your loins; fresh courage take;
Our God will never us forsake;
And soon we'll have this tale to tell —
All is well! all is well!

We'll find the place which God for us prepared,
  Far away in the West,
Where none shall come to hurt or make afraid;
  There the Saints will be blessed.
We'll make the air with music ring,
Shout praises to our God and King;
Above the rest these words we'll tell —
All is well! all is well.

And should we die before our journey's through,
  Happy day! all is well!
We then are free from toil and sorrow, too;
  With the just we shall dwell!
But if our lives are spared again
To see the Saints their rest obtain,
O how we'll make this chorus swell —
All is well! all is well!

—*William Clayton*

MEN give me some credit for genius. All the genius I have
lies in this: When I have a subject in hand, I study it profoundly.
Day and night it is before me. I explore it in all its bearings.
My mind becomes pervaded with it. Then the effort which I
make the people are pleased to call the fruit of genius. It is the
fruit of labor and thought.

—*Alexander Hamilton*

BEGIN. The rest is easy.

—Author Unknown

IF you don't know where you're going, any road will take you there.

—Old Saying

LIFE moves in one direction only —and each day we are faced with an actual set of circumstances, not with what might have been, not with what we might have done, but with what is, and with where we are now — and from this point we must proceed: not from where we were, not from where we wish we were — but from where we are.

—Richard L. Evans

EVEN if you are on the right track, you will get run over if you just stand there.

—Arthur Godfrey

CHOOSE well; your choice is brief, and yet endless.

—Johann Wolfgang von Goethe

RETREAT is what one does when he has to — just before he begins again.

—Richard L. Evans

LET men decide firmly what they will not do; then they will be free vigorously to do what they ought to do.

—Mencius

THERE is a tide in the affairs of men, which, taken at the flood, leads on to fortune; omitted, all the voyage of their life is bound in shallows and in misery.

—Shakespeare

IT is not only what we do, but also what we do not do, for which we are accountable.

—Moliére

NOTHING comes from nothing. Nothing ever could.

—Richard Rodgers

YOU get out of life what you put into it — that's the trouble!

—Arnold Glasow

NOT a day passes over the earth but men and women of no note do great deeds, speak great words, and suffer noble sorrows. Of these obscure heroes, . . . the greater part will never be known till that hour when many that were great shall be small, and the small great.

—Charles Reade

YOU never stub your toe standing still. The faster you go, the more chance there is of stubbing your toe, but the more chance you have of getting somewhere.

—Charles F. Kettering

THE great thing in this world is not so much where we stand, as in what direction we are moving.

—*Oliver Wendell Holmes*

WHENEVER you see a job to do, ask yourself these two questions: If not by me — by whom? If not now — when?

—*Arthur Lagueux*

THE business of life is to go forward.

—*Samuel Johnson*

IF we are ever in doubt what to do, it is a good rule to ask ourselves what we shall wish on the morrow that we had done.

—*Sir John Lubbock*

TO every man there openeth . . .
A High Way, and a Low
And every man decideth
The way his soul shall go.

—*John Oxenham*

❧ Part 5 ☙

Education, Ignorance; Books, Teaching, Learning

A teacher affects eternity; he can never tell where his influence stops.

—HENRY ADAMS

TO educate a man in mind and not in morals is to educate a menace to society.

—*Theodore Roosevelt*

MEN occasionally stumble over the truth, but most of them pick themselves up and hurry off as if nothing had happened.

—*Sir Winston Churchill*

IGNORANCE never settles a question.

—*Benjamin Disraeli*

THE future belongs to those who prepare for it.

—*Ralph Waldo Emerson*

WHAT is opportunity to the man who can't use it?

—*George Eliot*

IGNORANCE is dangerous, but knowledge without responsibility is more dangerous.

—*Bruce B. Clark*

THE end of education is to see men made whole, both in competence and in conscience. For to create the power of competence without creating a corresponding direction to guide the use of that power is bad education. Furthermore, competence will finally disintegrate apart from conscience.

—*John Sloan Dickey*

THE fact we must remember is that we are educating students for a world that will not be ours but will be theirs. Give them a chance to be heard.

—*Dr. Carlos P. Romulo*

TRUTH is knowledge of things as they are, and as they were, and as they are to come.

—*Doctrine & Covenants 93:24*

NOTHING is more terrible than to see ignorance in action.

—*Johann Wolfgang von Goethe*

MOST of the discussion of higher education in the United States is about money. Money is very important, but we ought to think once in a while about the things that money cannot do.

—*Robert M. Hutchins*

INTEGRITY without knowledge is weak and useless. Knowledge without integrity is dangerous and dreadful.

—*Samuel Johnson*

THE test of every religious, political, or educational system is the man it forms.

—*Author Unknown*

BUT whoso shall offend one of these little ones which believe in me, it were better for him that a millstone were hanged about his neck, and that he were drowned in the depth of the sea.

—*New Testament, Matthew 18:6*

HE that is taught only by himself has a fool for a master.

—*Ben Jonson*

TRUST no one to be your teacher . . . except he be a man of God, walking in his ways and keeping his commandments.

—*Book of Mormon, Mosiah 23:14*

IF a carpenter or a blacksmith should spoil a piece of material he is working upon, he could throw it aside and take another piece, but the teacher cannot do this with the eternal soul of the child.

—*Karl G. Maeser*

WITHOUT character — devoted, rugged strength of soul — no man has a right to teach. . . . The great teacher never fails to leave a profound mark on young men and women. . . . And this mark of greatness in its last analysis is always a moral one.

—*David Starr Jordan*

IT must be the aim of education to teach the citizen that he must first of all rule himself.

—*Winthrop A. Aldrich*

A man is but what he knoweth.

—*Francis Bacon*

EVERY home is perforce a good or bad educational center. It does its work in spite of every effort to shrink or supplement it. No teacher can entirely undo what it does, be that good or bad.

—*Ida Tarbell*

THE only thing more costly than education is ignorance.

—*Author Unknown*

THE teacher who is attempting to teach without inspiring the pupil with a desire to learn is hammering on cold iron.

—*Horace Mann*

NO matter where the body is, the mind is free to go elsewhere.

—*W. H. Davies*

AN open mind is all very well in its way, but it ought not to be so open that there is no keeping anything in or out of it. It should be capable of shutting its doors sometimes, or it may be found a little draughty.

—*Samuel Butler*

THE parents have a right to say that no teacher paid by their money shall rob their children of faith in God and send them back to their homes skeptical, or infidels, or agnostics, or atheists.

—*William Jennings Bryan*

THE worth of a book is to be measured by what you can carry away from it.

—*James Bryce*

THE very abundance of books in our days — a stupefying and terrifying abundance — has made it more important to know how to choose. . . . The first piece of advice I will venture to give you is this: Read only the best books. . . . Let not an hour . . . be wasted on third-rate or second-rate stuff if first-rate stuff can be had.

—*James Bryce*

WE talk of food for the mind, as of food for the body. Now a good book contains such food inexhaustible. . . . No book is worth anything which is not worth much.

—*John Ruskin*

WHEN I get a little money, I buy books; and if any is left, I buy food and clothes.

—*Erasmus*

BOOKS are the best of things, well used. Abused, among the worst.

—*Ralph Waldo Emerson*

EXCEPT a living man, there is nothing more wonderful than a book! a message to us from the dead — from human souls we never saw, who lived, perhaps thousands of miles away. And yet these, in those little sheets of paper, speak to us, arouse us, terrify us, teach us, comfort us, open their hearts to us as brothers.

—*Charles Kingsley*

SOME books are to be tasted, others to be swallowed, and some few to be chewed and digested.

—*Francis Bacon*

HE ate and drank the precious
    words,
His spirit grew robust;
He knew no more that he was poor,
Nor that his frame was dust.
He danced along the dingy days,
And this bequest of wings
Was but a book. What liberty
A loosened spirit brings!

—*Emily Dickinson*

WHEN you find that a book is poor . . . waste no more time upon it.

—*James Bryce*

NEXT to acquiring good friends, the best acquisition is that of a good book.

—*Charles Caleb Colton*

SEEK ye diligently and teach one another words of wisdom; yea, seek ye out of the best books words of wisdom; seek learning, even by study, and also by faith.

—*Doctrine & Covenants 88:118*

STUDY and learn, and become acquainted with all good books, and with languages, tongues, and people.

—*Doctrine & Covenants 90:15*

READING is . . . the royal road to intellectual eminence. . . . Truly good books are more than mines to those who can understand them. They are the breathings of the great souls of past times. Genius is not embalmed in them, but lives in them perpetually.

—*William Ellery Channing*

WHAT greater or better gift can we offer the republic than to teach and instruct our youth?

—*Cicero*

I conceive that books are like men's souls; divided into sheep and goats. Some few are going up, and carrying us up, heavenward; calculated, I mean, to be of priceless advantage in teaching, — in forwarding the teaching of all generations. Others, a frightful multitude, are going down, down; doing ever the more and the wider and the wilder mischief. Keep a strict eye on the latter class of book, my young friends!

—*Thomas Carlyle*

READING is to the mind what exercise is to the body. As by the one, health is preserved, strengthened and invigorated: by the other, virtue (which is the health of the mind) is kept alive, cherished and confirmed.

—*Joseph Addison*

IF I had my life to live over again, I would have made a rule to read some poetry and listen to some music at least once a week; for perhaps the parts of my brain now atrophied would thus have been kept active through use. The loss of these tastes is a loss of happiness.

—*Charles Darwin*

MORE than to give information, a teacher needs to help guide a student's mind to think, and even beyond that, to help him shape his character. Giving information is easy. Forming a thinking mind is hard. And shaping a strong character is hardest of all, partly because it must be shaped mostly from within. Giving information is only the beginning of a teacher's responsibility; the end is to stimulate, excite, motivate, lift, challenge, inspire.

—*Bruce B. Clark*

WE cannot be saved until we have risen above all our enemies, not the least of which is ignorance.

—*Joseph Smith*

THERE is an old proverb which says in substance: "He gives twice who gives quickly." It could be paraphrased to say, "He teaches twice who teaches early" — not when it is convenient only, not at some too long delayed a time, but when children are young, when they are with us, when they can be taught.

—*Richard L. Evans*

GOETHE once said of someone, "He is a dull man. If he were a book, I would not read him."

—*James Bryce*

WE are the children of that Being who lives in the heavens, who is filled with all intelligence, and possesses all power. We cannot be prepared to dwell with Him unless we instruct our minds and sanctify ourselves in all things.

—*Brigham Young*

WE need to add to the three R's, namely Reading, 'Riting and 'Rithmetic, a fourth — Responsibility.

—*Herbert Hoover*

YOUR students deserve more than your knowledge. They deserve and hunger for your inspiration. They want the warm glow of personal relationship. This always has been the hallmark of a great teacher.

—*Gordon B. Hinckley*

THE best guarantee against poor discipline is good teaching. . . . If the teaching is good enough, the students will be attentive and responsive. When students are bored and unruly, the best solution is not harsher rules but better teaching.

—*Bruce B. Clark*

HE who learns but does not think, is lost. He who thinks but does not learn, is in great danger.

—*Confucius*

THERE are some things you can give another person, and some things you cannot give him, except as he is willing to reach out and take them, and pay the price of making them a part of himself. This principle applies to studying, to developing talents, to absorbing knowledge, to acquiring skills, and to the learning of all the lessons of life.

—*Richard L. Evans*

O the vainness, and frailties, and the foolishness of men! When they are learned they think they are wise, and they hearken not unto the counsel of God, for they set it aside, supposing they know of themselves, wherefore, their wisdom is foolishness and it profiteth them not. And they shall perish. But to be learned is good if they hearken unto the counsels of God.

—*Book of Mormon, II Nephi 9:28-29*

THE greatest and noblest pleasure which men have in this world is to discover new truths, and the next is to shake off old prejudices.

—*Frederick the Great*

PROVE that you can control yourself and you are an educated man; and without this all other education is good for nothing.

—*Roswell Dwight Hitchcock*

WHAT the student is made to see and feel and sense, and every innuendo, is all part of the teaching process. To be a teacher *is* a sacred trust, and in a very real sense, the teacher is responsible for the total effect of his teaching.

—*Richard L. Evans*

A university must be a place of light, of liberty, and of learning.

—*Benjamin Disraeli*

GOD offers to every mind its choice between truth and repose.

Ralph Waldo Emerson

THE glory of God is intelligence, or, in other words, light and truth.

—*Doctrine & Covenants 93:36*

WHATEVER principle of intelligence we attain unto in this life, it will rise with us in the resurrection.

—*Doctrine & Covenants 130:18*

IT is impossible for a man to be saved in ignorance.

—*Doctrine & Covenants 131:6*

THE world was all forgot, the struggle o'er, Desperate the joy — that day they read no more.

—*Leigh Hunt*

FOR the guidance of all men in their choices in life let it be solemnly remembered that it is often easier to find the truth than to accept it.

—*Richard L. Evans*

EDUCATION for democracy must mean that every man must learn to think for himself.

—*Robert M. Hutchins*

IT matters little to me whether my pupil is intended for the army, the church, or the law. Before his parents chose a calling for him, nature called him to be a man. When he leaves me he will be neither a magistrate, nor a soldier, nor a priest. He will be a man.

—*Jean-Jacques Rousseau*

WE must be careful what we read and not, like the sailors of Ulysses, take bags of wind for sacks of treasures.

—*Sir John Lubbock*

EDUCATION does not mean teaching people to know what they do not know; it means teaching them to behave as they do not behave.

—*John Ruskin*

WHERE there is an open mind, there will always be a frontier.

—*Charles F. Kettering*

THERE is no darkness but ignorance.

—*Shakespeare*

SEEKERS and learners alike, banded together in the search for knowledge, will honor thought in all its finer ways, will welcome thinkers, . . . will uphold ever the dignity of thought and learning and will exact standards in these things.

—*John Masefield*

THE object of true education is to make people not merely do the right things but enjoy them.

—*John Ruskin*

THE great obligation upon a teacher is to be prepared to teach. A teacher cannot teach others that which he himself does not know. He cannot make his students feel what he does not feel himself.

—*David O. McKay*

AGAINST stupidity the Gods themselves contend in vain.

—*Friedrich Schiller*

CHARACTER development is the great, if not the sole, aim of education.

—*William James O'Shea*

THIS knowledge of truth, combined with proper regard for it, and its faithful observance, constitutes true education. The mere stuffing of the mind with a knowledge of facts is not education. The mind must not only possess a knowledge of truth, but the soul must revere it, cherish it, love it as a priceless gem; and this human life must be guided and shaped by it in order to fulfill its destiny.

—*Joseph F. Smith*

IT is only the ignorant who despise education.

—*Publius Syrus*

WHENEVER a student fails, a teacher fails also.

—*Bruce B. Clark*

FULLNESS of knowledge always and necessarily means some understanding of the depths of our ignorance, and that is always conducive to both humility and reverence.

—*Robert A. Millikan*

READ the best books first, or you may not have a chance to read them at all.

—*Henry David Thoreau*

I do not know what I may appear to the world, but to myself I seem to have been only like a boy playing on the seashore, and diverting myself in now and then finding a smoother pebble or a prettier shell than ordinary, whilst the great ocean of truth lay all undiscovered before me.

—*Sir Isaac Newton*

THE personal influence of the teacher, in moulding the character of his pupils, is the most important element in their education. In morals, a teacher cannot teach what he is not. If he talks what he is not, it were better not said, for his life talks more forcibly and is sooner believed both by children and adults.

W. M. Welch

WE shall never see the time when we shall not need to be taught.

—*Brigham Young*

WISDOM is the principal thing; therefore get wisdom; and with all thy getting get understanding.

—*Old Testament, Proverbs 4:7*

FROM a student to a teacher,

I bring to you the molten treasure of my mind
To cast and mold into some coinage of greater worth.
I've bound the wandering ways of youth
Down to the hard conformity of books.

But you have promised this:
Some day the metal that you pour
All base and crude into the crucible of study
Shall come forth a loveliness and satisfaction
Within your weary hands.

Well, mark you this:
I've trusted you; my youth and faith are yours.
I keep the pact. See to it that
You've told the truth.
                              —*Marba C. Josephson*

WHAT is a man,
If his chief good and market of his time
Be but to sleep and feed? A beast, no more.
Sure He that made us with such large discourse,
Looking before and after, gave us not
That capability and god-like reason
To fust in us unus'd.
                              —*Shakespeare (from Hamlet)*

ALL true wisdom that mankind have they have received from
God, whether they know it or not. There is no ingenious mind
that has ever invented anything beneficial to the human family
but what he obtained it from that One Source, whether he knows
or believes it or not. There is only one source from whence men
obtain wisdom, and that is God, the fountain of all wisdom, and
though men may claim to make their discoveries by their own
wisdom, by meditation and reflection, they are indebted to our
Father in heaven for all.
                              —*Brigham Young*

THE dangers of knowledge are not to be compared with the dangers of ignorance.

—*Richard Whately*

TIS education forms the common mind:
Just as the twig is bent, the tree's inclined.

—*Alexander Pope*

WHATEVER I did not know, I was not ashamed to inquire about, so I acquired knowledge.

—*Ancient Persian Philosopher*

LIVE always in the best company when you read.

—*Sydney Smith*

WE might ask, when shall we cease to learn? I will give you my opinion about it; never, never.

—*Brigham Young*

IGNORANCE is a voluntary misfortune.

—*Nicholas Ling*

TO learn what is true in order to do what is right is the summing up of the whole duty of man.

—*Thomas Henry Huxley*

WHOSO neglects learning in his youth loses the past, and is dead for the future.

—*Euripides*

EDUCATION is the power to think clearly, the power to act well in the world's work, and the power to appreciate life.

—*Brigham Young*

IGNORANCE is not innocence, but sin.

—*Robert Browning*

THERE are obviously two educations. One should teach us how to make a living, and the other how to live.

—*James Truslow Adams*

EDUCATION does not commence with the alphabet. It begins with a mother's look and a father's nod and a sister's gentle pressure on the hand and a brother's act of forbearance. With flowers and green dells and on hills with birds' nests admired but not touched, with pleasant walks in shady lanes, with thoughts directed in sweet and kindly tones, with deeds of virtue and benevolent thoughts to the source of all good and to God Himself.

—*Author Unknown*

WE pray for wisdom, but God will as soon put bread and meat in our cupboards without any endeavor of ours, as he will give us wisdom without our trying to get it.

—*Brigham Young*

TRUE education does not consist merely in the acquiring of a few facts of science, history, literature, or art; but in the development of character. True education awakens a desire to conserve health by keeping the body clean and undefiled. True education trains in self-denial and self-mastery. True education regulates the temper, subdues passion and makes obedience to social laws and moral order a guiding principle of life. It develops reason and inculcates faith in the living God as the eternal, loving Father of all.

—*David O. McKay*

SOME never learn anything because they know everything too soon.

—*Author Unknown*

THERE is nothing so stupid as an educated man, if you get him off the thing he was educated in.

—*Will Rogers*

THE end of all knowledge should be in virtuous action.

—*Sir Philip Sidney*

IT does not matter so much *what* your daughter studies as under *whom* she studies.

—*W. M. Welch*

THE man who does not read good books has no advantage over the man who can't read them.

—*Mark Twain*

A man is saved no faster than he gets knowledge.

—*Joseph Smith*

A man is not paid for having brains but for using them.

—*Author Unknown*

IF you were graduated yesterday, and have learned nothing today, you will be uneducated tomorrow.

—*Author Unknown*

FORTUNE favors the best prepared people.

—*Author Unknown*

Law, Liberty;
Commandments,
Government,
Judgement,
and Justice

Heaven is above all yet; there sits a judge that no king can corrupt.

—SHAKESPEARE

THE world no longer has a choice between force and law. If civilization is to survive it must choose the rule of law.

—*Dwight D. Eisenhower*

IT is the common fate of the indolent to see their rights become a prey to the active. The condition upon which God has given liberty to man is eternal vigilance.

—*John Philpot Curran*

OUR nation was founded as an experiment in human liberty. Its institutions reflect the belief of our founders that men had their origin and destiny in God; that they were endowed by Him with inalienable rights and had duties prescribed by moral law, and that human institutions ought primarily to help men develop their God-given possibilities.

—*John Foster Dulles*

LIBERTY will not descend to a people; a people must raise themselves to liberty; it is a blessing that must be earned before it can be enjoyed.

—*Charles Caleb Colton*

IS life so dear, or peace so sweet, as to be purchased at the price of chains and slavery? Forbid it, Almighty God! I know not what course others may take; but as for me, give me liberty or give me death!

—*Patrick Henry*

THE curse of ages will rest upon you if ever you surrender to domestic lawlessness the precious liberties for which your fathers bled.

—*John Mitchell Mason*

DON'T you think the Ten Commandments should be rewritten?" "No, re-read."

—*Author Unknown*

EVERY generation a new crop of fools comes on. They think they can beat the orderly universe. They conceive themselves to be more clever than the eternal laws. They snatch goods from Nature's store, and run. . . . And one by one they all come back to Nature's counter, and pay — pay in tears, in agony, in despair; pay as fools before them have paid. . . . Nature keeps books pitilessly. Your credit with her is good, but she collects; there is no land you can flee to and escape her bailiffs. . . . She never forgets; she sees to it that you pay her every cent you owe, with interest.

—Dr. Frank Crane

NO man is above the law and no man is below it; nor do we ask any man's permission when we require him to obey it.

—Theodore Roosevelt

THERE is a law, irrevocably decreed in heaven before the foundations of this world, upon which all blessings are predicated — And when we obtain any blessing from God, it is by obedience to that law upon which it is predicated.

—Doctrine & Covenants 130:20-21

THOU shalt love the Lord thy God with all thy heart, and with all thy soul, and with all thy mind. This is the first and great commandment. And the second is like unto it, Thou shalt love thy neighbour as thyself.

—New Testament, Matthew 22:37-39

EVERY step we take toward making the State the caretaker of our lives, by that much we move toward making the State our master.

—Dwight D. Eisenhower

WE are too inclined to think of law as something merely restrictive — something hemming us in. We sometimes think of law as the opposite of liberty. But this is a false conception. . . . God does no contradict Himself. He did not create man and then, as an afterthought, impose upon him a set of arbitrary, irritating, restrictive rules. He made man free — and then gave him commandments to keep him free. . . . We cannot break the Ten Commandments. We can only break ourselves against them — or else, by keeping them, rise through them to the fulness of freedom under God. God means us to be free. With divine daring, He gave us the power of choice.

—Cecil B. DeMille

THOU shalt have no other Gods before me.

Thou shalt not make unto thee any graven image. . . .

Thou shalt not bow down thyself to them, nor serve them. . . .

Thou shalt not take the name of the Lord thy God in vain. . . .

Remember the sabbath day, to keep it holy.

Honour thy father and thy mother: that thy days may be long
upon the land which the Lord thy God giveth thee.

Thou shalt not kill.

Thou shalt not commit adultery.

Thou shalt not steal.

Thou shalt not bear false witness. . . .

Thou shalt not covet thy neighbour's house . . .
thy neighbour's wife . . . nor anything else that is
thy neighbour's.

—Old Testament, Exodus 20:3-17
The Ten Commandments

IF men were angels, no government would be necessary. . . . In framing a government which is to be administered by men over men, the great difficulty lies in this: you must first enable the government to control the governed; and in the next place oblige it to control itself.

—James Madison

BLESSED is the nation whose God is the Lord.

—Old Testament, Psalm 33:12

WE hold these truths to be self-evident, that all men are created equal, that they are endowed by their Creator with certain unalienable Rights, that among these are Life, Liberty, and the pursuit of Happiness.

—From The Declaration of Independence

THE American Constitution is, so far as I can see, the most wonderful word ever struck off at a given time by the brain and purpose of man.

—William E. Gladstone

WE the people of the United States, in order to form a more perfect Union, establish justice, insure domestic tranquility, provide for the common defense, promote the general welfare, and secure the blessings of liberty to ourselves and our posterity, do ordain and establish this Constitution of the United States of America.

*—From the Preamble to the
Constitution of the
United States of America*

THE constitution of the United States is a glorious standard . . . founded in the wisdom of God . . . established . . . by the hands of wise men . . . raised up unto this very purpose. It is to all those who are privileged with the sweets of liberty like the cooling shades and refreshing waters of a great rock in a thirsty and weary land.

—Joseph Smith

THE laws and constitution of the people . . . should be maintained for the rights and protection of all flesh, according to just and holy principles; that every man may act . . . according to the moral agency . . . given unto him, that every man may be accountable for his own sins in the day of judgment.

—Doctrine & Covenants 101:77-78

CHOOSE you this day whom ye will serve; . . . but as for me and my house, we will serve the Lord.

—Old Testament, Joshua 24:15

WE believe that governments were instituted of God for the benefit of man; and that he holds men accountable for their acts in relation to them, both in making laws and administering them, for the good and safety of society. We believe that no government can exist in peace, except such laws are framed and held inviolate as will secure to each individual the free exercise of conscience, the right and control of property, and the protection of life.

—Doctrine & Covenants 134:1-2

FOURSCORE and seven years ago our fathers brought forth upon this continent a new nation, conceived in liberty, and dedicated to the proposition that all men are created equal. Now we are engaged in a great civil war, testing whether that nation, or any nation so conceived and so dedicated, can long endure. We are met on a great battlefield of that war. We have come to dedicate a portion of that field as a final resting-place for those who here gave their lives that that nation might live. It is altogether fitting and proper that we should do this. But in a larger sense we cannot dedicate, we cannot consecrate, we cannot hallow this ground. The brave men, living and dead, who struggled here, have consecrated it far above our poor power to add or detract. The world will little note, nor long remember, what we say here; but it can never forget what they did here. It is for us, the living, rather to be dedicated here to the unfinished work which they who fought here have thus far so nobly advanced. It is rather for us to be here dedicated to the great task remaining before us, that from these honored dead we take increased devotion to that cause for which they gave the last full measure of devotion; that we here highly resolve that these dead shall not have died in vain; that this nation, under God, shall have a new birth of freedom, and that government of the people, by the people, and for the people, shall not perish from the earth.

—Abraham Lincoln, "Gettysburg Address"

HE hath shewed thee, O man, what is good; and what doth the Lord require of thee, but to do justly, and to love mercy, and to walk humbly with thy God?

—Old Testament, Micah 6:8

FREEDOM cannot live after the family as we know it is dead. Freedom cannot out-live morality.

—Thomas Anderson

FEAR God, and keep his commandments: for this is the whole duty of man.

—Old Testament, Ecclesiastes 12:13

NO free government can stand without virtue in the people, and a lofty spirit of patriotism. . . . Thank God my life has been spent in a land of liberty.

—Andrew Jackson

THERE is no liberty to men who know not how to govern themselves.

—*Henry Ward Beecher*

THE law of the harvest is inexorable. As we sow, so shall we reap.

—*Hugh B. Brown*

WE believe that religion is instituted of God; and that men are amenable to him, and to him only, for the exercise of it, unless their religious opinions prompt them to infringe upon the rights and liberties of others; but we do not believe that human law has a right to interfere in prescribing rules of worship to bind the consciences of men, nor dictate forms for public or private devotion; that the civil magistrate should restrain crime, but never control conscience; should punish guilt, but never suppress the freedom of the soul.

—*Doctrine & Covenants 134:4*

ALL that is necessary for the triumph of evil is that good men do nothing.

—*Edmund Burke*

THERE'S too much talk about enforcing laws and not enough said about obeying them.

—*Arnold Glasow*

LIBERTY is always dangerous, but it is the safest thing we have.

—*Harry Emerson Fosdick*

FOR behold, it is not meet that I should command in all things; for he that is compelled in all things, the same is a slothful and not a wise servant; wherefore he receiveth no reward. Verily I say, men should be anxiously engaged in a good cause, and do many things of their own free will, and bring to pass much righteousness; For the power is in them, wherein they are agents unto themselves. And inasmuch as men do good they shall in nowise lose their reward. But he that doeth not anything until he is commanded, and receiveth a commandment with doubtful heart, and keepeth it with slothfulness, the same is damned.

—*Doctrine & Covenants 58:26-29*

JUDGE not according to the appearance, but judge righteous judgment. . . . For with what judgment ye judge, ye shall be judged: and with what measure ye mete, it shall be measured to you again.

—*New Testament, John 7:24;*
Matthew 7:2

LIBERTY cannot be established without morality, nor morality without faith.

—*Horace Greeley*

WHAT is liberty without wisdom and without virtue?

—*Edmund Burke*

WE stand for preservation of our heritage through obedience to law.

—*Mormon Youth Group Motto*

TO suppose that our civil and political liberties are secure because they are abstractly defined in written constitutions is to mistake the legal form for the living substance of freedom.

—*Carl Lotus Becker*

IT is not right that any man should be in bondage one to another.

—*Doctrine & Covenants 101:79*

OBEDIENCE is the mother of success, the wife of safety.

—*Aeschylus*

DEMOCRACY is the worst system ever invented — except for all the rest.

—*Sir Winston Churchill*

THE true danger is, when liberty is nibbled away, for expedients, and by parts.

—*Edmund Burke*

SO long as Faith with Freedom reigns . . . and men are free to think and act, life is worth living still.

—*Alfred Austin*

THE arm of the law is only as long as the alertness of its citizens.

—*Richard L. Evans*

WHERE liberty dwells, there is my country.

—*John Milton*

AS a fatigue falls on a community, the citizens are less inclined for that eternal vigilance which has truly been called the price of liberty; and they prefer to arm only one single sentinel to watch the city while they sleep.

—*Gilbert Keith Chesterton*

AND, if you keep my commandments and endure to the end you shall have eternal life, which gift is the greatest of all the gifts of God.

—*Doctrine & Covenants 14:7*

THOSE who know the truth are not equal to those who love it, and those who love it are not equal to those who live it.

—*Confucius*

MAN has changed again and again, but the mandates from God are still the same as they have always been because the fundamental principles of good behavior are immutable.

—*David Lawrence*

DEMOCRACY is not something which can be inherited. It is a process which must be worked upon and then re-worked upon continuously.

—*C. A. Dykstra*

THERE is no liberty in wrongdoing. It chains and fetters its victim as surely as effect follows cause.

—*Joseph Cook*

FREEDOM is a God-given inalienable right, and is essential to the soul's salvation in the highest sense. And every man must be protected in his right to choose as to certain essentials. But when we flout any law — of society, of the land, of nature, or of God — we pay a price. We reap the results of the seeds we sow. Freedom can be used or abused, but there is this certainty concerning it: freedom cannot keep us from consequences.

—Richard L. Evans

THE battle, Sir, is not to the strong alone; it is to the vigilant, the active, the brave.

—Patrick Henry

ONE lesson, and only one, history may be said to repeat with distinctness; that the world is built somehow on moral foundations; that in the long run it is well with the good; in the long run it is ill with the wicked.

—James A. Froude

I have the utmost sympathy for any person who has never had a decent chance in life. But the fact that society has treated him badly does not give him the right to smash store windows and take what he wants, or to attack our police with animal ferocity. This is heading toward an era of lawlessness, which in the end can only lead to anarchy. And anarchy is a destroyer of nations.

—Dwight D. Eisenhower

WE must remember that we have to make judges out of men, and that by being made judges their prejudices are not diminished and their intelligence is not increased.

—Robert G. Ingersoll

IF a nation values anything more than freedom it will lose its freedom; and the irony of it is that if it is comfort or money that it values more, it will lose that too.

—William Somerset Maugham

BY the rude bridge that arched the flood,
　　Their flag to April's breeze unfurled,
Here once the embattled farmers stood,
　　And fired the shot heard round the world.

*　　*　　*

Spirit, that made those spirits dare
　　To die, and leave their children free,
Bid Time and Nature gently spare
　　The shaft we raise to them and thee.

—Ralph Waldo Emerson

TIS with our judgments as our watches: none go just alike, yet each believes his own.

—Alexander Pope

A State which dwarfs its men, in order that they may be more docile instruments in its hands — even for beneficial purposes — will find that with small men no great thing can really be accomplished.

—John Stuart Mill

WILLING conformity to law gives man his finest freedom.

—Richard L. Evans

ONE fact stands out in bold relief in the history of men's attempts for betterment. That is that when compulsion is used, only resentment is aroused, and the end is not gained. Only through moral suasion and appeal to men's reason can a movement succeed.

—Samuel Gompers

MY son, keep thy father's commandment, and forsake not the law of thy mother: Bind them continually upon thine heart, and tie them about thy neck. When thou goest, it shall lead thee; when thou sleepest, it shall keep thee; and when thou awakest, it shall talk with thee.

—Old Testament, Proverbs 6:20-22

GOOD intentions will always be pleaded for every assumption of power. It is hardly too strong to say that the Constitution was made to guard the people against the dangers of good intentions.

—Daniel Webster

HE who shall introduce into public affairs the principles of a primitive Christianity, will change the face of the world.

—Benjamin Franklin

A man has need of tough ears to hear himself fairly judged.

—Montaigne

EDWARD Gibbon, in 1788, set forth in his famous book, "Decline and Fall of the Roman Empire," five basic reasons why that great civilization withered and died:

1. The undermining of the dignity and sanctity of the home, which is the basis for human society. 2. Higher and higher taxes: the spending of public money for free bread and circuses for the populace. 3. The mad craze for pleasure, with sports and plays becoming more exciting, more brutal and more immoral. 4. The building of great armaments when the real enemy was within — the decay of individual responsibility. 5. The decay of religion, whose leaders lost their touch with life, and their power to guide the people.

No man has a right to do as he pleases, except when he pleases to do right.

—*Charles Simmons*

There are two freedoms, the false where one is free to do what he likes, and the true where he is free to do what he ought.

—*Charles Kingsley*

Human nature will not change. In any future great national trial, compared with the men of this, we shall have as weak and as strong, as silly and as wise, as bad and as good.

—*Abraham Lincoln*

One man's word is no man's word. We should quietly hear both sides.

—*Johann Wolfgang von Goethe*

Let reverence of the law be breathed by every mother to the lisping babe. . . . Let it be taught in schools, . . . seminaries, and colleges; let it be written in primers, spelling books, and almanacs; let it be preached from pulpits, and proclaimed in legislative halls, and enforced in courts of justice; let it become the political religion of the nation.

—*Abraham Lincoln*

The first law that ever God gave to man was a law of obedience.

—*Montaigne*

There is not an individual upon the earth but what has within himself ability to save or to destroy himself; and such is the case with nations.

—*Brigham Young*

What is the best government? — That which teaches us to govern ourselves.

—*Johann Wolfgang von Goethe*

Government is not reason, it is not eloquence — it is a force. Like fire, it is a dangerous servant and a fearful master.

—*George Washington*

Nothing has an uglier look to us than reason, when it is not on our side.

—*Lord Halifax*

If men be good, government cannot be bad.

—*William Penn*

Of a surety at the Day of Judgment it will be demanded of us, not what we have read, but what we have done; not how well we have spoken, but how holily we have lived. In all that thou doest, remember the end, and how thou wilt stand before a strict judge, from whom nothing is hid, who is not bribed with gifts, nor accepteth excuses, but will judge righteous judgment.

—*Thomas á Kempis*

LIBERTY lies in the hearts of men and women. When it dies there, no constitution, no law, no court can save it.

—*Judge Learned Hand*

GOD of our fathers, known of old—
Lord of our far-flung battle line—
Beneath Whose awful hand we hold
Dominion over palm and pine—
Lord God of Hosts, be with us yet,
Lest we forget—lest we forget!

—*Rudyard Kipling*

THE greatest glory of a freeborn people is to transmit that freedom to their children.

—*William Harvard*

GIVE therefore thy servant an understanding heart . . . for who is able to judge . . . ?

—*Old Testament, I Kings 3:9*

THE spirit of liberty is the spirit of Him who, nearly 2,000 years ago, taught mankind a lesson that it has never learned, but has never quite forgotten: that there may be a kingdom where the least shall be heard and considered side by side with the greatest.

—*Judge Learned Hand*

LAWLESS are they that maketh their wills their law.

—*Shakespeare*

BAD men cannot make good citizens. It is when a people forget God that tyrants forge their chains. A vitiated state of morals, a corrupted public conscience, is incompatible with freedom. No free government, or the blessings of liberty, can be preserved to any people but by a firm adherence to justice, moderation, temperance, frugality, and virtue; and by a frequent recurrence to fundamental principles.

—*Patrick Henry*

WHAT I do say is, that no man is good enough to govern another man without that other's consent.

—*Abraham Lincoln*

YOU have the highest of human trusts committed to your care. Providence has showered on this favored land blessings without number, and has chosen you, as the guardians of freedom, to preserve it for the benefit of the human race. May He who holds in His hands the destinies of nations make you worthy of the favors He has bestowed, and enable you, with pure hearts, and pure hands, and sleepless vigilance, to guard and defend to the end of time the great charge He has committed to your keeping.

—*Andrew Jackson*

I believe there are more instances of the abridgment of the freedom of the people by gradual and silent encroachment of those in power than by violent and sudden usurpations.

—*James Madison*

WE claim the privilege of worshiping Almighty God according to the dictates of our own conscience, and allow all men the same privilege, let them worship how, where or what they may.

—*Joseph Smith*

I have sworn upon the altar of God eternal hostility against every form of tyranny over the mind of man.

—*Thomas Jefferson*

THEY will be vanquished by their vices as easily as by force of arms.

—*Tacitus*

WHAT is it to you if a man is such and such, if another does or says this or that? You will not have to answer for others, but you will have to give an account of yourself.

—*Thomas á Kempis*

IT isn't always others who enslave us. Sometimes we let circumstances enslave us; sometimes we let routine enslave us; sometimes we let things enslave us; sometimes, with weak wills, we enslave ourselves. Sometimes we partake of detrimental things that we think will soothe our nerves, minds, or imaginations — things we think will help us to escape from reality. But no man is free if he is running away from reality. And no man is free if he is running away from himself.

—*Richard L. Evans*

OUR defense is in the spirit which prizes liberty as the heritage of all men in all lands everywhere. Destroy this spirit and you will have planted the seeds of despotism at our own doors. . . . Whether it is right or wrong to trample on the rights of others — that is the real issue . . . the eternal struggle between the two principles of right and wrong throughout the world.

—*Abraham Lincoln*

NO nation can remain free unless its people cherish their freedoms, understand the responsibilities they entail, and nurture the will to preserve them. Law is the strongest link between man and freedom.

—*John F. Kennedy*

NO one is ever innocent, when his opponent is the judge.

—*Lucan*

I ask you — is God, who the scriptures say is the same yesterday, today and forever, now changing His mind? Does Jesus no longer believe what He taught when He was on earth? For any man to attempt to change the moral law is like trying to change the Deity Himself.

—*Mark E. Petersen*

TO obey God is perfect liberty; he that does this shall be free, safe, and quiet.

—*Seneca*

LEAN liberty is better than fat slavery.

—*John Ray*

TRUE liberty consists in the privilege of enjoying our own rights, not in the destruction of the rights of others.

—*George Pinckard*

THERE is no act, however trivial, but has its train of consequences.

—*Samuel Smiles*

IT'S home again, and home again,
    America for me!
I want a ship that's westward bound
    to plough the rolling sea,
To the blessed Land of Room Enough
    beyond the ocean bars,
Where the air is full of sunlight and
    the flag is full of stars.

—*Henry Van Dyke*

LET us turn our thoughts on the character of our country.

—*Charles Sumner*

WE believe in being subject to kings, presidents, rulers, and magistrates, in obeying, honoring, and sustaining the law.

—*Joseph Smith*

CHANCE is a word void of sense; nothing can exist without a cause.

—*Voltaire*

THE history of liberty is a history of the limitations of governmental power, not the increase of it.

—*Woodrow Wilson*

REASON and experience both forbid us to expect that national morality can prevail in exclusion of religious principle.

—*George Washington*

I, the Lord, am bound when ye do what I say; but when ye do not what I say, ye have no promise.

—*Doctrine & Covenants 82:10*

HE who feels that his own opinion is his law is not a safe citizen.

—*Richard L. Evans*

NATURE is the expression of a definite order with which nothing interferes successfully, and the chief business of men is to learn that order and govern themselves accordingly.

—*Author Unknown*

KNOW this, that every soul is free
To choose his life and what he'll be;
For this eternal truth is given,
That God will force no man to heaven.

He'll call, persuade, direct aright,
And bless with wisdom, love and light;
In nameless ways be good and kind,
But never force the human mind.

—*William C. Gregg*

I teach them correct principles, and they govern themselves.

—*Joseph Smith*

LET no man break the laws of the land, for he that keepeth the laws of God hath no need to break the laws of the land.

—*Doctrine & Covenants 58:21*

WITH how little wisdom the world is governed.

—*Author Unknown*

REMEMBER that any government which gets so big that it can give you everything you want will also be so big that it can take everything you've got!

—*William Miller*

ONLY the disciplined are free.

—*James C. Penney*

IF ever you make a mistake of judgment, let it be on the side of mercy.

—*Joseph Fielding Smith*

WHERE the Spirit of the Lord is, there is liberty.

—*New Testament, II Corinthians 3:17*

CONFIRM thy soul in self-control, thy liberty in law.

—*Katherine Lee Bates*

OUR Father's God, to thee,
Author of liberty,
    To thee we sing.
Long may our land be bright
With freedom's holy light.
Protect us by thy might,
    Great God, our King!

—*Samuel F. Smith*

❧ Part 7 ❧

Birth, Life, Health and Time

Our birth is but a sleep and a forgetting:
The soul that rises with us, our life's star,
Hath had elsewhere its setting,
And cometh from afar:
Not in entire forgetfulness,
And not in utter nakedness,
But trailing clouds of glory do we come
From God, who is our home:
Heaven lies about us in our infancy!

—WILLIAM WORDSWORTH

NOTHING that has an end is long.

—*Cicero*

LIFE is too short to be little.

—*Benjamin Disraeli*

DON'T waste time. Don't waste it in idleness; don't waste it in regretting the time already wasted; don't waste it in dissipation; don't waste it in resolutions a thousand times repeated, never to be carried out. Don't waste your time. Use all of it. Sleep, work, rest, think.

—*Arthur Brisbane*

SPEND your time in nothing which you know must be repented of.

—*Richard Baxter*

HUMAN life is something that comes to us from beyond this world, and the purpose of our society is to cherish it and enable the individual to attain the highest achievement of which he is capable. Human life is God-given and infinitely valuable.

—*Harry S. Truman*

TO every thing there is a season, and a time to every purpose under the heaven: A time to be born, and a time to die; a time to plant, and a time to pluck up that which is planted; A time to kill, and a time to heal; a time to break down, and a time to build up; A time to weep, and a time to laugh; a time to mourn, and a time to dance; A time to cast away stones, and a time to gather stones together; a time to embrace, and a time to refrain from embracing; A time to get, and a time to lose; a time to keep, and a time to cast away; A time to rend, and a time to sew; a time to keep silence, and a time to speak; . . . He hath made every thing beautiful in his time.

—Old Testament, Ecclesiastes 3:1-8, 11

MAN must not allow the clock and the calendar to blind him to the fact that each moment of his life is a miracle and a mystery.

—H. G. Wells

THERE'S a time for some things,
    and a time for all things;
A time for great things,
    and a time for small things.

—Cervantes

WE live in deeds, not years; in thoughts, not breaths; in feelings, not in figures on a dial. We should count time by heart-throbs. He most lives who thinks most, feels the noblest, acts the best.

—Phillip James Bailey

LIFE is what happens to you while you are making other plans.

—A. J. Marshall

LIFE is like playing a violin solo in public and learning the instrument as one goes on.

—Samuel Butler

SOME folks in this world spend their whole time hunting after righteousness and can't find any time to practice it.

—Josh Billings

YOU will never "find" time for anything. If you want time you must make it.

—Charles Buxton

ANY machine, whether the human body or an automobile, will obviously wear out sooner if it is overworked, mistreated, improperly lubricated or fed chemicals that leave a residue of carbon around the valves! So treat your marvelous human machine far more carefully than a Rolls Royce!

—Dr. George W. Crane

PHILOSOPHERS have explained space. They have not explained time. It is the inexplicable raw material of everything. With it, all is possible; without it, nothing. The supply of time is truly a daily miracle. . . . You wake up in the morning, and . . . your purse is magically filled with twenty-four hours. . . . It is yours. It is the most precious of possessions. . . . And no one receives either more or less than you receive. . . . Moreover, you cannot draw on the future. . . . You can only waste the passing moment. You cannot waste tomorrow; it is kept for you. You cannot waste the next hour; it is kept for you. . . . You have to live on this twenty-four hours of daily time. Out of it you have to spin health, pleasure, money, content, respect, and the evolution of your immortal soul. Its right use, its most effective use, is a matter of highest urgency. . . . All depends on that.

—Arnold Bennett

MY father early gave me to understand that a sound and serviceable body was essential for a happy and productive life.

—Samuel A. Eliot

CHOOSE rather to punish your appetites than to be punished by them.

—Tyrius Maximus

THE fulness of the earth is yours. . . . Yea, all things which come of the earth, in the season thereof, are made for the benefit and the use of man, both to please the eye and to gladden the heart, . . . to strengthen the body and to enliven the soul.

—Doctrine & Covenants 59:16-19

THE preservation of health is a duty. Few seem conscious that there is such a thing as physical morality.

—Herbert Spencer

ONE cannot conceive of a parent's not being interested in everything that pertains to his children: their physical, mental, moral and spiritual health, and happiness. And one cannot conceive of the Father of us all not being interested in everything that pertains to His children.

—Richard L. Evans

DOES not health mean harmony? A healthy body is good; but a soul in right health, — it is the thing beyond all others to be prayed for; the blessedest thing this earth receives of Heaven.

—Thomas Carlyle

TOBACCO is not . . . good for man, . . .

—Doctrine & Covenants 89:8

EVEN nectar is poison if taken to excess.

—Hindu Proverbs

AVOID late and unseasonable Studies, for they murder Wit and are very prejudicial to Health. The Muses love the Morning, and that is a fit Time for Study. After you have din'd, either divert yourself at some Exercise, or take a Walk, and discourse merrily, and Study between whiles. As for Diet, eat only as much as shall be sufficient to preserve Health, and not as much or more than the Appetite may crave. Before Supper, take a little Walk, and do the same after Supper. A little before you go to sleep read something that is exquisite, and worth remembering; and contemplate upon it till you fall asleep; and when you awake in the Morning, call yourself to an Account for it.

—Erasmus

TEMPERANCE and labor are the two best physicians; the one sharpens the appetite, the other prevents indulgence to excess.

—Jean-Jacques Rousseau

DO I use food and drink in no other sort and in no other degree than was designed by Him who gave these [things] for our sustenance? Do I never abuse my body by inordinate labor, striving to accomplish some end which I have unwisely proposed? Do I use action enough in some useful employ, or do I sit too much idle while some persons who labor to support me have too great a share of it? If in any of these things I am deficient, to be incited to consider it is a favor to me.

—John Woolman

THE human body, in its wonderful structure, is of itself a miracle of divine wisdom and power.

—Author Unknown

WINE is a mocker, strong drink is raging: and whosoever is deceived thereby is not wise.

—Old Testament, Proverbs 20:1

FOR Time will teach thee soon the truth,
There are no birds in last year's nest!

—Henry Wadsworth Longfellow

LIFE is always opening new and unexpected things for us. There is no monotony in living to him who walks . . . with open and perceptive eyes. The monotony of life, if life is monotonous to you, is in you, not in the world.

—Phillips Brooks

SIMPLICITY and straightforwardness are . . . in the power of all of us.

—Henry Alford

LIFE is not a goblet to be drained; it is a measure to be filled.

—Author Unknown

A man who dares to waste one hour of life has not discovered the value of life.

—Charles Darwin

ALL wholesome herbs God hath ordained for the constitution, nature, and use of man — Every herb in the season thereof, and every fruit in the season thereof; all these to be used with prudence and thanksgiving. . . . All grain is ordained for the use of man and of beasts, to be the staff of life, not only for man but for the beasts of the field, and the fowls of heaven, and all wild animals that run or creep on the earth. . . . All grain is good for the food of man; as also the fruit of the vine; that which yieldeth fruit, whether in the ground or above the ground — Nevertheless, wheat for man, and corn for the ox, and oats for the horse, and rye for the fowls and for swine, and for all beasts of the field, and barley for all useful animals, and for mild drinks, as also other grain. And all saints who remember to keep and do these sayings, walking in obedience to the commandments, shall receive health in their navel and marrow to their bones; And shall find wisdom and great treasures of knowledge, even hidden treasures; And shall run and not be weary, and shall walk and not faint.

—Doctrine & Covenants 89:10-20

LOOK over the world, Is it not wonderful , . . . if your eyes were open! This Earth, God made it for you; appointed paths in it; you can live in it; go to and fro on it.

—Thomas Carlyle

IT takes courage to live — courage and strength and hope and humor.

—Jerome Fleishman

WRITE it on your heart that every day is the best day in the year. . . . Finish every day, and be done with it. You have done what you could.

—Ralph Waldo Emerson

MAY you live all the days of your life.

—Jonathan Swift

NOTHING but a good life here can fit men for a better one hereafter.

—William Penn

THE future is something which everyone reaches at the rate of sixty minutes an hour, whatever he does, whoever he is.

—Clive Staples Lewis

I have given you life — now make the most of it.

—Author Unknown

WHILE the earth remaineth, seedtime and harvest, and cold and heat, and summer and winter, and day and night shall not cease.

—Old Testament, Genesis 8:22

EACH of us here, let the world go how it will . . . has he not a Life of his own to lead? . . . The world's being saved will not save us; nor the world's being lost destroy us. We should look to ourselves.

—*Thomas Carlyle*

GOD asks no man whether he will accept life. That is not the choice. You *must* take it. The only choice is *how*.

—*Henry Ward Beecher*

THOUGH we seem grieved at the shortness of life in general, we are wishing every period of it at an end. The minor longs to be at age, then to be a man of business, then to make up an estate, then to arrive at honors, then to retire.

—*Joseph Addison*

MODERATION is the silken string running through the pearl-chain of all virtues.

—*Thomas Fuller*

THE wise man will always reflect concerning the quality, not the quantity of life.

—*Seneca*

LIFE consists in what man is thinking of all day.

—*Ralph Waldo Emerson*

THE best thing about the future is that it comes only one day at a time.

—*Abraham Lincoln*

HAPPY, vivid and full of interest as it has been, I do not seek to tread again the toilsome and dangerous path. Not even an opportunity of making a different set of mistakes and experiencing a different series of adventures and successes would lure me. How can I tell that the good fortune which has up to the present attended me with fair constancy would not be lacking at some critical moment in another chain of causation.

—*Sir Winston Churchill*

THIS time, like all times, is a very good one, if we but know what to do with it.

—*Ralph Waldo Emerson*

LIFE will give you what you ask of her if only you ask long enough and plainly enough.

—*Author Unknown*

NO life ever grows great until it is focused, dedicated, and disciplined.

—*Harry Emerson Fosdick*

THERE is more to life than increasing its speed.

—*Mahatma Gandhi*

LIFE can only be understood backwards; but it must be lived forwards.

—*Soren Kierkegaard*

THERE is no point in quaking with the impact of every hour. We have to have faith, the faith to quiet our hearts in the midst of confusion and uncertainties. We can't run away from everything; we can't keep on running from anything — for sooner or later we would run out of the strength to run. We have to live life, face it, honor it, enjoy it, adjust to it.

—*Richard L. Evans*

I have one advice to give you, . . . remember the care of health. I have no doubt you have among you young souls ardently bent to consider life cheap, for the purpose of getting forward in what they are aiming at on high; but you are to consider, that health is a thing to be attended to continually. . . . What to it are nuggets and millions?

—*Thomas Carlyle*

AS long as you live, keep learning how to live.

—*Seneca*

THE past isn't here to speak for itself and hence gets a better reputation than it deserves.

—*Author Unknown*

I still find each day too short for all the thoughts I want to think, all the walks I want to take, all the books I want to read, and all the friends I want to see.

—*John Burroughs*

DOTH thou love life? Then do not squander time, for that is the stuff life is made of.

—*Benjamin Franklin*

THIS I know well: that the chief part of every life consists of small things. . . . Blessed is the man who can enjoy the small things, the common beauties, the little day-by-day events; sunshine on the fields, birds on the bough, breakfast, dinner, supper, the daily paper on the porch, a friend passing by. So many people who go afield for enjoyment leave it behind them at home.

—*David Grayson*

THIS is life — and it is passing. What are we waiting for?

—*Richard L. Evans*

THE business of life is to go forward.

—*Samuel Johnson*

THE measure of life is not length, but honesty.

—*John Lyly*

NOTHING is swifter than the years.

—*Ovid*

NOW good is man's life, the mere living! how fit to employ
All the heart and the soul and the senses forever in joy!

—*Robert Browning*

TODAY is your day and mine, the only day we have, the day in which we play our part. What our part may signify in the great whole, we may not understand; but we are here to play it, and now is our time. This we know: it is a part of action, not of whining. It is a part of love, not cynicism. It is for us to express love in terms of human helpfulness.

—*David Starr Jordan*

THAT . . . illimitable, silent, never-resting thing called Time, rolling, rushing on, swift, silent, like an all-embracing ocean-tide.

—*Thomas Carlyle*

THERE is no wealth but life.

—*John Ruskin*

LEARN to make the most of life,
Lose no happy day,
Time will never bring thee back
Chances swept away!

Leave no tender word unsaid,
Love while love shall last;
"The mill cannot grind
With the water that is past."

—*Sarah Doudney*

MY way is to begin with the beginning.

—*Lord Byron*

OH, how much good time you lose over a bad matter!

—*Seneca*

DON'T wish for each part of life to be past. Despite all the problems and the pressures, enjoy the journey. It's a good world and a good life — God made it so, and it is up to us to find the sweetness in it, to find what we can of heaven here, until we arrive, with our loved ones, at that heaven which is everlastingly hereafter.

—*Richard L. Evans*

YOU may delay, but time will not.

—*Benjamin Franklin*

LIFE, like every other blessing, derives its value from its use alone.

—*Samuel Johnson*

I do not have to make over the universe; I have only to do my job, great or small, and to look often at the trees and the hills and the sky, and be friendly with all men.

—*David Grayson*

THE time is out of joint: O cursed spite,
That ever I was born to set it right!

—*Shakespeare*

BELIEVE that life is worth living and your belief will create the fact.

—*William James*

THE tragedy of life is what dies inside a man while he lives.

—*Albert Schweitzer*

So he died for his faith. That is fine,
  More than most of us do.
But, say, can you add to that line
  That he lived for it, too?

In his death he bore witness at last
  As a martyr to the truth.
Did his life do the same in the past,
  From the days of his youth?

It is easy to die. Men have died
  For a wish or a whim,
From bravado or passion or pride.
  Was it harder for him?

But to live — every day to live out
  All the truth that he dreamt,
While his friends met his conduct with doubt
  And the world with contempt.

Was it thus that he plodded ahead,
  Never turning aside?
Then we'll talk of the life that he lived.
  Never mind how he died.

—Ernest Crosby

A sense of purpose and the opportunity to contribute to others — these are as vital to total health as are adequate nutrition and rest.

—H. A. Holle

As if you could kill time without injuring eternity!

—Henry David Thoreau

Time is much like manna: We can't hoard it. We can't save it. The Lord allots each day its own supply.

—Richard L. Evans

Nothing is more unworthy of a wise man, or ought to trouble him more, than to have allowed more time for trifling and useless things than they deserved.

—Plato

The life given us by nature is short; but the memory of a well-spent life is eternal.

—Cicero

If time be of all things the most precious, let us then be up and doing, and doing to the purpose.

—Benjamin Franklin

THERE is an eternity behind and an eternity before, and this little speck in the center, however long, is comparatively but a minute.

—*John Brown*

WE are, all of us, a reflection of what we do with time, of what we want — or at least what we want enough to be willing to work for.

—*Richard L. Evans*

OBEDIENCE to Law, Respect for Others, Mastery of Self, Joy in Service — these constitute life.

—*Author Unknown*

TIME is the most valuable thing that a man can spend.

—*Diogenes*

THE inaudible and noiseless foot of Time.

—*Shakespeare*

LIFE is a stream that moves us silently, certainly, with no stopping place for any of us as we move through time and eternity, with each one to be what he can, and do what he can, through the whole length of life.

—*Richard L. Evans*

O my young friends, the world is beautiful and . . . life is full of promise.

—*Phillips Brooks*

TO be able to look back on one's past life with satisfaction is to live twice.

—*Marcus Valerius Martialis*

A sound head, an honest heart, and a humble spirit are the three best guides through time and to eternity.

—*Sir Walter Scott*

LOSE none of the Time that is yet thine . . . since without it we can do nothing in this World . . . [and] God will certainly most strictly reckon with us, when Time shall be no more.

—*William Penn*

WHY is there never enough time
    to do it *right*
But always enough time to do it over?

—*Author Unknown*

THIS speck of life in time's great
    wilderness
This narrow isthmus 'twixt two boundless seas,
The past, the future, two eternities!

—*Thomas Moore*

ALL the world's a stage, and all
The men and women merely players;
They have their exits and their entrances,
And one man in his time plays many
    parts . . .

—*Shakespeare*

OUT of the shadows of night
The world rolls into light;
It is daybreak everywhere.

—Henry Wadsworth Longfellow

ONLY one life to live! We all want to do our best with it. We all want to make the most of it. What is worth while? . . . The question of life is not, How much time have we? — for in each day each of us has exactly the same amount: we have 'all there is.' The question is, What shall we do with it? . . . Time spent in being interrupted is not time lost. . . . There is time enough given us to do all that God means us to do each day and to do it gloriously! How do we know but that the interruption we snarl at is the most blessed thing that has come to us in long days?

—Anna R. Lindsay

CONSCIOUS of the fact that I cannot separate myself from the time in which I am living, I have decided to become a part of it.

—Albert Camus

I hate people who are always running down the future because that's where I am going to spend the rest of my life.

—Charles F. Kettering

YEARS following years steal something every day.
At last they steal us from ourselves away.

—Horace

IN three words I can sum up everything I've learned about life: It goes on.

—Robert Frost

THE moving finger writes; and, having writ,
Moves on; nor all your piety nor wit
    Shall lure it back to cancel half a line,
Nor all your tears wash out a word of it.

—Omar Khayyam

I want to be thoroughly used before I die, and I want to die gloriously solvent, intellectually, morally, and financially.

—Omar Bernard Shaw

HUMBLE voyagers are we,
    O'er Life's dim, unsounded sea,
Seeking only some calm clime;
    Touch us gently, gentle Time.

—Bryan Waller Procter

THE future is that time when
You'll wish you'd done
What you aren't doing now!

—Author Unknown

WHEN in the beginning of the years,
God mixed in man the raptures and the tears
And scattered thru his brain the starry stuff,
He said, "Behold! Yet this is not enough,
For I must test his spirit to make sure.
That he can dare the vision and endure.

"I will withdraw my face,
Veil me in shadow for a certain space,
And leave behind only a broken clue,
A crevice where the glory shimmers thru,
Some whisper from the sky,
Some footprints in the road to track me by.

"I will leave man to make the fateful guess,
Will leave him torn between the no and yes,
Leave him unresting till he rests in me,
Drawn upward by the choice that makes him free,
Leave him in tragic loneliness to choose,
With all in life to win or all to lose."

—*Edwin Markham*

NOTHING that is can pause or stay;
The moon will wax, the moon will wane,
The mist and cloud will turn to rain,
The rain to mist and cloud again,
    To-morrow be to-day.

—*Henry Wadsworth Longfellow*

Part 8

Death and Everlasting Life

**Night never had the last word.
The dawn is always invincible.**

—Hugh B. Brown

So nature deals with us, and takes away our playthings one by one, and by the hand leads us to rest.

—*Henry Wadsworth Longfellow*

We miss thy small step on the stair;
We miss thee at thine evening prayer;
All day we miss thee, everywhere.

—*David Macbeth Moir*

At first when you were gone I turned my face
From life and sat upon a lonely place
Apart from men, bewailed but nursed my sorrow
And, loving yesterday, I loathed tomorrow.

Then suddenly you said, "O foolish one,
Awake, there are no dead — I *am* your own!"
And then above my sorrow and my strife
I found the Resurrection and the Life.

—*Robert Norwood*

Those who hope for no other life are dead even for this.

—*Johann Wolfgang von Goethe*

We are born for a higher destiny than that of earth.

—*Edward G. Bulwer-Lytton*

I am sure that some of you who think yourselves very modern, nonchalant about death and what lies after it, may some day run abruptly into an experience which will shake you to the depths. Somebody whom you love, the most priceless soul, it may be, you ever have loved, will die, and you will find that you cannot say that you are not interested, do not care, that it makes no difference to you what lies beyond death for that personality.

—*Harry Emerson Fosdick*

So live, that when thy summons comes to join
The innumerable caravan, which moves
To that mysterious realm where each shall take
His chamber in the silent halls of death —
Thou go not like the quarry-slave at night,
Scourged to his dungeon. But, sustained and soothed
By an unfaltering trust, approach thy grave
Like one who wraps the drapery of his couch
About him, and lies down to pleasant dreams.

—*William Cullen Bryant*

No cogent reason remains for supposing the soul dies with the body. . . . We [scientists] find strong reasons for believing that man is of extraordinary importance in the cosmic scheme. . . . It takes a lifetime to build the character of a noble man. The exercise and discipline of youth, the struggles and failures of maturity, the loneliness and tranquility of age — these make the fire through which he must pass to bring out the pure gold of his soul. Having been thus perfected, what shall Nature do with him, annihilate him? What infinite waste! As long as there is in heaven a God of love there must be for God's children *everlasting life!*

—*Dr. Arthur H. Compton*
(1928 Nobel Prize winner in Physics)

I don't care what they say with their mouths — everybody knows that something is eternal. And it ain't houses and it ain't names, and it ain't earth, and it ain't even the stars — everybody knows in their bones that something is eternal, and that something has to do with human beings. All the greatest people who ever lived have been telling us that for five thousand years and yet you'd be surprised how people are always losing hold of it. There's something way down deep that's eternal about every human being.

—*Thornton Wilder*

FOR notwithstanding they die, they also shall rise again.

—*Doctrine & Covenants 88:27*

FOR Death is no more than a Turning of us over from Time to Eternity.

—*William Penn*

BEGIN to be now what you will be hereafter.

—*St. Jerome*

IS death the last sleep? No, it is the last and final awakening.

—*Sir Walter Scott*

NO man can be ignorant that he must die, nor be sure that he may not this very day.

—*Cicero*

NOW cracks a noble heart. Good night, sweet prince; And flights of angels sing thee to thy rest!

—*Shakespeare*

YOUR mother closed her eyes in peaceful slumber, and awakened with loved ones.

—*David O. McKay*

LET us accustom ourselves to regard death as a form of life which we do not yet understand; . . . Death is but . . . a departure into an unknown filled with wonderful promises.

—*Maurice Maeterlinck*

LIFE is eternal; and love is immortal; and death is only a horizon; and a horizon is nothing save the limit of our sight.

—*Rossiter Worthington Raymond*

WHEN I consider the wonderful activity of the mind, so great a memory of what is past, and such capacity for penetrating the future; when I behold such a number of arts and sciences, and such a multitude of discoveries, . . . I believe and am firmly persuaded that a nature which contains so many things within itself cannot but be immortal.

—*Cicero*

BE still prepared for death: and death or life shall thereby be the sweeter.

—*Shakespeare*

THOSE who leave us are welcomed by others.

—*Richard L. Evans*

SHE is not dead, — the child of
    our affection, —
But gone unto that school
Where she no longer needs our poor
    protection,
And Christ himself doth rule.

In that great cloister's stillness and
    seclusion,
By guardian angels led,
Safe from temptation, safe from sin's
    pollution,
She lives, whom we call dead.

Day after day we think what she is
    doing
In those bright realms of air;
Year after year, her tender steps
    pursuing,
Behold her grown more fair.

Thus do we walk with her, and keep
    unbroken
The bond which nature gives,
Thinking that our remembrance,
    though unspoken,
May reach her where she lives.

—*Henry Wadsworth Longfellow*

OH, God! it is a fearful thing
To see the human soul take wing.

—*Lord Byron*

IT matters not at what hour the righteous fall asleep. Death cannot come untimely to him who is fit to die. The less of this cold world, the more of heaven; the briefer life, the earlier immortality.

—*Henry Hart Milman*

WHEN she had passed, it seemed like the ceasing of exquisite music.

—*Henry Wadsworth Longfellow*

DO not suppose, my dearest ones, that when I have left you I shall be nowhere and no one. Even when I was with you, you did not see my soul, but knew that it was in this body of mine from what I did. Believe then that it is still the same, even though you see it not. . . . Wherefore, . . . preserve my memory by the loyalty and piety of your lives.

—*Cicero*

AREN'T you glad that God didn't leave all the details to us?

—*Robert L. Simpson*

DEATH is not a subject for mourning when it is followed by immortality.

—*Cicero*

WE sometimes congratulate ourselves at the moment of waking from a troubled dream: it may be so the moment after death.

—*Nathaniel Hawthorne*

A little way to walk with you my own,
    only a little way,
Then one of us must weep and walk alone
    until God's day.

—*Frank L. Stanton*

SUNSET and evening star,
    And one clear call for me,
And may there be no moaning of the bar,
    When I put out to sea.

But such a tide as moving seems asleep,
    Too full for sound and foam,
When that which drew from out the boundless deep
    Turns again home.

Twilight and evening bell,
    And after that the dark!
And may there be no sadness of farewell,
    When I embark;

For tho' from out our bourne of time and place
    The flood may bear me far,
I hope to see my Pilot face to face
    When I have crossed the bar.

—*Alfred Lord Tennyson*

WHEN sinks the soul, subdued by toil to slumber,
    Its closing eyes look up to thee in prayer,
Sweet the repose beneath thy wings o'ershading
    But sweeter still to wake and find thee there.

So shall it be at last in that bright morning
    When the soul waketh, and life's shadows flee,
O in that hour, fairer than daylight's dawning,
    Shall rise the glorious thought, I am with thee —
Still, still with thee.

—*Harriet Beecher Stowe*

DOES the journey seem long,
The path rugged and steep?
Are there briars and thorns on the way?
Do sharp stones cut your feet
As you struggle to rise
To the heights through the heat of the day?

Is your heart faint and sad,
Your soul weary within,
As you toil 'neath your burden of care?
Does the load heavy seem
You are forced now to lift?
Is there no one your burden to share?

Let your heart be not faint
Now the journey's begun;
There is One who still beckons to you.
Look upward in gladness
And take hold of his hand,
He will lead you to heights that are new.

—*Joseph Fielding Smith*

THE crash of the whole solar and stellar systems could only kill you once.

—*Thomas Carlyle*

THE question whether our conscious personality survives after death has been answered by almost all races of men in the affirmative.

—*Sir James Frazer*

DEATH hath ten thousand several doors
For men to take their exit.

—*John Webster*

WHO that hath ever been
Could bear to be no more?
Yet who would tread again the scene
He trod through life before?

—*James Montgomery*

IT is a poor thing for anyone to fear that which is inevitable.

—*Tertullian*

FOR God so loved the world, that he gave his only begotten Son, that whosoever believeth in him should not perish, but have everlasting life.

—*New Testament, John 3:16*

THE truest end of life is to know the Life that never ends.

—*William Penn*

ALL that is, at all,
Lasts ever, past recall;
Earth changes, but thy soul and God stand sure.
What entered into thee,
That was, is, and shall be.

—*Robert Browning*

DEATH is the liberator of him whom freedom cannot release; the physician of him whom medicine cannot cure; the comforter of him whom time cannot console. .

—*Charles Caleb Colton*

WHEN a man is as old as I am, he is bound occasionally to think about death. In my case this thought leaves me in perfect peace, for I have a firm conviction that our spirit is a being indestructible by nature. It works on from eternity; it is like the sun which only seems to set, but in truth never sets but shines on unceasingly.

—*Johann Wolfgang von Goethe*

THE memory of an individual is written in indelible script in space and time.

—*Dr. Gustaf Stromberg*

TO find the loved ones waiting on the shore,
More beautiful, more precious than before.

—*Ella Wheeler Wilcox*

AS to] our future beyond the grave, it is in no way necessary that we should have an answer to everything. . . . Total annihilation is impossible. . . . Neither a body nor a thought can drop out of the universe, out of time and space. . . . For there is no place where anything ceases to be. . . . To be able to do away with a thing — that is to say, to fling it into nothingness — nothingness would have to exist, and if it exists, under whatever form, it is no longer nothingness.

—*Maurice Maeterlinck*

SEEMS it strange that thou shouldst live forever? Is it less strange that thou shouldst live at all?

—*Edward Young*

I know of nobody that has a mind to die this year.

—*Thomas Fuller*

DEATH is as the foreshadowing of life. We die that we may die no more.

—*Herman Hooker*

WE picture death as coming to destroy; let us rather picture Christ as coming to save. We think of death as ending; let us rather think of life as beginning, and that more abundantly. We think of losing; let us think of gaining. We think of parting, let us think of meeting. We think of going away; let us think of arriving. And as the voice of death whispers "You must go from earth," let us hear the voice of Christ saying, "You are but coming to ME!"

—*Norman Macleod*

THEY that love beyond the world cannot be separated by it. Death cannot kill what never dies. Nor can spirits ever be divided that love and live in the same divine principle, the root and record, of their friendship.

—*William Penn*

DEATH is the golden key that opens the palace of eternity.

—*John Milton*

HE is not dead,
Your son, your dear beloved son,
Your golden one,
With his blond tousled head,
The shining and excited words he said!
Ah no! Be comforted.
For him the world will never
Grow flat and tired and dull;
He is a part of all swift things forever,
All joyous things that run
Or fly,
Familiar to the wind and cloud and sky,
Forever beautiful!

—*Joseph Austlander*

THEY were lovely and pleasant in their lives, and in death they were not divided.

—*Author Unknown*

COME as you are . . . but come *now!*

—*Lindsay R. Curtis*

LET death be daily before your eyes, and you will never entertain any abject thought, nor too eagerly covet anything.

—*Epictetus*

DEATH and love are the two wings that bear the good man to heaven.

—*Michelangelo*

ALL mankind is of one author, and is one volume; when one man dies, one chapter is not torn out of the book, but translated into a better language; and every chapter must be so translated. God employs several translators; some pieces are translated by age, some by sickness, some by war, some by justice; but God's hand is in every translation, and his hand shall bind up all our scattered leaves again for that library where every book shall lie open to one another.

—*John Donne*

WHEN would we be willing to leave those we love?

—*Richard L. Evans*

NO man is an island entire of itself; every man is a piece of the continent, a part of the main. If a clod be washed away by the sea, Europe is the less, as well as if a promontory were, as well as if a manor of thy friend's or of thine own were. Any man's death diminishes me, because I am involved in mankind, and therefore never send to know for whom the bell tolls; it tolls for thee.

—*John Donne*

EACH departed friend is a magnet that attracts us to the next world.

—*Jean Paul Richter*

ONCE more the Heavenly Power Makes all things new, . . .

—*Alfred Lord Tennyson*

LIFE! we've been long together
Through pleasant and through cloudy
weather.
It's hard to part when friends are
dear,—
Perhaps it will cost a sigh, a tear;
—Then steal away, give little warning,
Choose thine own time: Say not good-
night—
But—some brighter time
Bid me good morning.

—Anna L. Barbauld

WE understand death for the first
time when he puts his hand upon one
whom we love.

—Madame de Stael

O God, my Father, while I stray
Far from my path on life's rough way,
O teach me from my heart to say,
Thy will, O God, Thy will be done.

Tho' dark my path and sad my lot,
Let me be still and murmur not;
But breathe the prayer divinely taught,
Thy will, O God, Thy will be done.

If Thou shouldst call me to resign
What most I prize, it ne'er was mine.
I only yield Thee what is Thine.
Thy will, O God, Thy will be done.

—Author Unknown

I tell you they have not died; . . .
They live, they know, they see:
They shout with every breath:
All is Eternal life! There is no death!

—Gordon Johnstone

PRAISE Him that He died for men:
Praise Him that He rose again.

—Joseph Anstice

I am the resurrection, and the life:
he that believeth in me, though he
were dead, yet shall he live:
And whosoever liveth and believeth in
me shall never die.

—New Testament, John 11:25-26

TOMB, thou shalt not hold him
longer;
Death is strong, but Life is stronger;
Stronger than the dark, the light;
Stronger than the wrong, the right;
Faith and Hope triumphant say
Christ will rise on Easter Day.

—Phillips Brooks

OUR Lord has written the promise
of the resurrection, not in books alone,
but in every leaf in springtime.

—Martin Luther

AND so make life, and death, and
that vast forever
One grand sweet song.

—Charles Kingsley

THOU shalt live together in love,
insomuch that thou shalt weep for the
loss of them that die, and more especially for those that have not hope of
a glorious resurrection.

—Doctrine and Covenants 42:45

FEAR death?—to feel the fog in my throat
    The mist in my face,
When the snows begin, and the blasts denote
    I am nearing the place,
The power of the night, the press of the storm,
    The post of the foe;
Where he stands, the Arch Fear in a visible form,
    Yet the strong man must go;
For the journey is done and the summit attained,
    And the barriers fall,
Though a battle's to fight ere the guerdon be gained,
    The reward of it all.
I was ever a fighter, so — one fight more,
    The best and the last!
I would hate that death bandaged my eyes, and forbore,
    And bade me creep past.
No! let me taste the whole of it, fare like my peers,
    The heroes of old,
Bear the brunt, in a minute pay glad life's arrears
    Of pain, darkness, and cold.
For sudden the worst turns the best to the brave,
    The black minute's at end,
And the elements that rage, the fiend-voices that rave:
    Shall dwindle, shall blend,
Shall change, shall become first a peace out of pain,
    Then a light, then thy breast,
O thou soul of my soul! I shall clasp thee again,
    And with God be the rest!

—*Robert Browning, Prospice*

LIFE is real! Life is earnest!
    And the grave is not its goal;
Dust thou art, to dust returnest,
    Was not spoken of the soul.

—*Henry Wadsworth Longfellow*

WHICH is the more difficult, to be born, or to rise again?

—*Blaise Pascal*

THE only way to take the sorrow out of death is to take love out of life.

—*Author Unknown*

ONE short sleep past, we wake eternally,
And Death shall be no more: Death, thou shalt die!

—*John Donne*

WHEN God sends forth a tiny soul
    To learn the ways of earth,
A mother's love is waiting here —
    We call this wonder — birth.

When God calls home a tired soul
    And stills a fleeting breath,
A Father's love is waiting there,
    This too is birth — not death.

—Author Unknown

ANYTHING less than infinity is too small. Anything less than eternity or immortality is too short.

—Author Unknown

BEHOLD, he that hath eternal life is rich.

—Doctrine & Covenants 6:7

I decline to accept the end of man. It is easy enough to say that man is immortal simply because he will endure. . . . I believe that man will not merely endure: he will prevail. He is immortal, not because he alone among creatures has an inexhaustible voice, but because he has a soul, a spirit capable of compassion and sacrifice and endurance.

—William Faulkner

ELSE what shall they do which are baptized for the dead, if the dead rise not at all? Why are they then baptized for the dead?

—New Testament, I Corinthians 15:29

IF in this life only we have hope in Christ, we are of all men most miserable.

—New Testament, I Corinthians 15:19

IT is impossible that anything so natural, so necessary, and so universal as death should ever have been designed by Providence as an evil to mankind.

—Jonathan Swift

GOD'S finger touched him, and he slept.

—Alfred Lord Tennyson

ASK the winds that blow which leaf on the tree will be next to go.

—An Old Proverb

HEAVEN will not be heaven to me if I do not meet my wife there.

—Andrew Jackson

AY! it will come, — the bitter hour! but bringing
    A better love beyond, more subtle-sweet;
A higher road to tread, with happier singing,
    And no cross-ways to part familiar feet!

—Sir Edwin Arnold

FOR as in Adam all die, even so in Christ shall all be made alive.

—*New Testament, I Corinthians 15:22*

SO when a great man dies,
For years beyond our ken,
The light he leaves behind him lies
Upon the paths of men.

—*Charles Sumner*

DON'T be sad.
  I'm not leaving.
    I'm arriving.

—*last words of Gaby Morlay*
(French Actress)

THERE is a future, O thank God!

—*Henry de Lafayette Webster*

PEACE I leave with you,
My peace I give unto you:
Not as the world giveth,
Give I unto you.
Let not your heart be troubled,
Neither let it be afraid.

In my Father's house are many mansions:
If it were not so, I would have told you.
I go to prepare a place for you.

And if I go and prepare a place for you,
I will come again and receive you unto myself;
That where I am, ye may be also.
And whither I go ye know,
And the way ye know.

Peace I leave with you.
My peace I give unto you.

—*New Testament*
(Adapted from John 14:2-4, 27)

Part 9

Faith, Prayer; God, and His Word

**The fool hath said in his heart,
There is no God.**

—OLD TESTAMENT, PSALM 14:1

ALL I have seen teaches me to trust the Creator for all I have not seen.

—*Ralph Waldo Emerson*

I know this world is ruled by Infinite Intelligence. It required Infinite Intelligence to create it and it requires Infinite Intelligence to keep it on its course. . . . It is mathematical in its precision.

—*Thomas A. Edison*

I would rather walk with God in the dark than go alone in the light.

—*Mary Gardiner Brainard*

THE more I try to unravel the mysteries of the world we live in, the more I come to the conception of a single overruling power — God.

—*Henry Eyring*

IT is not permitted us to know everything.

—*Horace*

I never saw a moor,
I never saw the sea;
Yet know I how the heather looks,
And what a wave must be.

I never spoke with God,
Nor visited in Heaven;
Yet certain am I of the spot
As if the chart were given.

—*Emily Dickinson*

THE disease with which the human mind now labors is want of faith.

—*Ralph Waldo Emerson*

WHEN a load of bricks, dumped on a corner lot, can arrange themselves into a house; when a handful of springs and screws and wheels, emptied onto a desk, can gather themselves into a watch, then and not until then will it seem sensible, to some of us at least, to believe that all these thousands or millions of worlds could have been created, balanced and set to revolving in their separate orbits, all without any directing intelligence at all.

—*Bruce Barton*

MAN is greater than a world — than systems of worlds; there is more mystery in the union of soul with the body, than in the creation of a universe.

—*Henry Giles*

BELIEVE in God; believe that he is, and that he created all things, both in heaven and in earth; believe that he has all wisdom, and all power, both in heaven and in earth; believe that man doth not comprehend all the things which the Lord can comprehend.

—*Book of Mormon, Mosiah 4:9*

I am the way, the truth, and the life: no man cometh unto the Father, but by me.

—*New Testament, John 14:6*

EPOCHS of faith are epochs of fruitfulness; but epochs of unbelief are barren.

—*Johann Wolfgang von Goethe*

IF radio's slim fingers can pluck a melody
From night — and toss it over a continent or sea;
If the petalled white notes of a violin
Are blown across the mountains or the city's din;
If songs, like crimson roses, are culled from thin blue air —
Why should mortals wonder if God hears prayer?

—*Ethel Romig Fuller*

FROM that time many of his disciples went back, and walked
no more with him.
Then said Jesus unto the twelve, "Will ye also go away?"
Then Simon Peter answered him, "Lord, to whom shall we go?
thou hast the words of eternal life.
And we believe and are sure that thou art that Christ, the Son of
the living God."

—*New Testament, John 6:66-69*

IT made me shiver, and I about made up my mind to pray and see if I couldn't try to quit bein' the kind of boy I was and be better. So I kneeled down. But the words wouldn't come. Why wouldn't they? It weren't no use to try and hide it from Him. . . . I knowed very well why they wouldn't come. It was because my heart wasn't right; it was because I was playin' double. I was lettin' on to give up sin, but way inside of me I was holdin' on to the biggest one of all. I was tryin' to make my mouth say I would do the right thing and the clean thing, but deep down in me I knowed it was a lie and He knowed it. You can't pray a lie. I found that out.

—Mark Twain
(Words of Huckelberry Finn)

FAITH is the assurance of things hoped for, and the conviction of things not seen.

—New Testament, Hebrews 11:1
(Revised Version)

THE most welcomed people of the world are never those who continually look back upon the trials, the sorrows, the failures, the bitter frustrations of yesterday, but those who cast their eyes forward with faith, hope, . . . courage, happy curiosity.

—James Francis Cooke

GOD is the silent partner in all great enterprises.

—Abraham Lincoln

IN all my perplexities and distresses, the Bible has never failed to give me light and strength.

—Robert E. Lee

I am absolutely unshaken in my faith that God created us, loves us, and wants us not only to be good but to be happy.

—Archibald Rutledge

MAN is certainly stark mad; he cannot make a worm, and yet he will be making gods by the dozens.

—Montaigne

WE account the Scriptures of God to be the most sublime philosophy. I find more sure marks of authority in the Bible than in any profane history whatever.

—Sir Isaac Newton

FAITH is the root of all good works; a root that produces nothing is dead.

—Daniel Wilson

A perfect faith would lift us absolutely above fear.

—George Macdonald

PRAYER is the soul's sincere desire,
  Uttered or unexpressed,
The motion of a hidden fire
  That trembles in the breast.

Prayer is the burden of a sigh,
  The falling of a tear,
The upward glancing of an eye,
  When none but God is near.

Prayer is the simplest form of speech
  That infant lips can try,
Prayer, the sublimest strains that reach
  The Majesty on high.

Prayer is the contrite sinner's voice,
  Returning from his ways,
While angels in their songs rejoice,
  And cry, "Behold, he prays!"

Nor prayer is made on earth alone:
  The Holy Spirit pleads,
And Jesus at the Father's throne,
  For sinners intercedes.

Oh, thou by whom we come to God,
  The Life, the Truth, the Way!
The path of prayer thyself hast trod;
  Lord, teach us how to pray.

—*James Montgomery*

FOR man's well-being, Faith is properly the one thing needful; how, with it, Martyrs, otherwise weak, can cheerfully endure the shame and the cross; and without it, Worldlings puke-up their sick existence, by suicide, in the midst of luxury.

—*Thomas Carlyle*

I have lived, seen God's hand through a lifetime, and all was for the best.

—*Robert Browning*

THE existence of the Bible, as a Book for the people, is the greatest benefit which the human race has ever experienced.

—*Immanuel Kant*

NOTHING in life is more wonderful than faith — the one great moving force which we can neither weigh in the balance nor test in the crucible.

—*Sir William Osler*

ABIDE with me; 'tis eventide!
  The day is past and gone;
The shadows of the evening fall;
  The night is coming on!
Within my heart a welcome guest,
  Within my home abide;
O Savior, stay this night with me;
  Behold, 'tis eventide!

Abide with me; 'tis eventide!
  Thy walk today with me
Has made my heart within me burn,
  As I communed with thee.
Thy earnest words have filled my soul
  And kept me near thy side;
O Savior, stay this night with me;
  Behold, 'tis eventide!

Abide with me; 'tis eventide!
  And lone will be the night,
If I cannot commune with thee,
  Nor find in thee my light.
The darkness of the world, I fear,
  Would in my home abide;
O Savior, stay this night with me;
  Behold, 'tis eventide!

—*M. Lowrie Hofford*

GOD is still the best medicine that we physicians can ever prescribe. But He expects us to team up with Him and utilize our wits, plus all the available drugs and other techniques that scientists have developed.

"God helps those who help themselves" is an old adage, which means that He doesn't want us lazily to ask Him to do all the curing when we have . . . other proved aids.

But when we get out of our depth, God often steps in and produces miraculous cures, as every experienced physician can attest.

—*Dr. George W. Crane*

AND now, after the many testimonies which have been given of him, this is the testimony, last of all, which we give of him: That he lives! For we saw him, even on the right hand of God; and we heard the voice bearing record that he is the Only Begotten of the Father—That by him, and through him, and of him, the worlds are and were created, and the inhabitants thereof are begotten sons and daughters unto God.

—*Doctrine & Covenants 76:22-24*

I consider an intimate knowledge of the Bible an indispensable qualification of a well-educated man.

—*Robert A. Millikan*

DON'T be a cynic, don't waste yourself in rejection.

—*Ralph Waldo Emerson*

IT is difficult to make a man miserable while he feels he is worthy of himself and claims kindred to the great God who made him.

—*Abraham Lincoln*

I need thee every hour,
　Most gracious Lord;
No tender voice like thine
　Can peace afford.

I need thee every hour,
　Stay thou nearby;
Temptations lose their power
　When thou art nigh.

I need thee every hour,
　In joy or pain;
Come quickly and abide,
　Or life is vain.

I need thee; O I need thee;
　Every hour I need thee!
O bless me now, my Savior;
　I come to thee!

—*Annie S. Hawkes*

WE don't know what water is. We don't know what electricity is. We don't know what heat is. We have a lot of hypotheses about these things, but that is all. But we do not let our ignorance about these things deprive us of their use.

—*Thomas A. Edison*

THERE never was found, in any age of the world, either religion or law that did so highly exalt the public good as the Bible.

—*Francis Bacon*

LEAD, kindly Light, amid the encircling gloom;
    Lead Thou me on!
The night is dark, and I am far from home;
    Lead Thou me on!
Keep Thou my feet; I do not ask to see
The distant scene — one step enough for me.

I was not ever thus, nor prayed that Thou
    Shouldst lead me on.
I loved to choose and see my path; but now
    Lead Thou me on!
I loved the garish day, and, spite of fears,
Pride ruled my will. Remember not past years.

So long Thy power hath blessed me, sure it still
    Will lead me on,
O'er moor and fen, o'er crag and torrent, till
    The night is gone;
And with the morn those angel faces smile
Which I have loved long since, and lost awhile.

—John Henry Newman

GIVE diligent heed to the words of eternal life. For you shall live by every word that proceedeth forth from the mouth of God.

—Doctrine & Covenants 84:43-44

THE son can do nothing of himself, but what he seeth the Father do.

—New Testament, John 5:19

IF a clock proves the existence of a clockmaker, and the world does not prove the existence of a Supreme Architect, then I consent to be called a fool.

—Voltaire

I said to the man who stood at the gate of the year: Give me a light that I may tread safely into the unknown: And he replied: Go out into the darkness and put thine hand into the hand of God. That shall be to thee better than light and safer than a known way.

—M. Louis Haskins

HE who has ceased to pray has lost a great friendship.

—Richard L. Evans

I don't believe scientists have discovered anything that God didn't already know.

—Harold B. Lee

GOD moves in a mysterious way
  His wonders to perform;
He plants his footsteps in the sea
  And rides upon the storm.

Deep in unfathomable mines
  Of never failing skill,
He treasures up his bright designs
  And works his sovereign will.

Ye fearful Saints, fresh courage take;
  The clouds ye so much dread
Are big with mercy and shall break
  In blessings on your head.

Judge not the Lord by feeble sense,
  But trust him for his grace;
Behind a frowning providence
  He hides a smiling face.

His purposes will ripen fast,
  Unfolding every hour;
The bud may have a bitter taste,
  But sweet will be the flower.

Blind unbelief is sure to err
  And scan his works in vain;
God is his own interpreter,
  And he will make it plain.

—*William Cowper*

AFTER reading the doctrines of Plato, Socrates, or Aristotle we feel that the specific difference between their words and Christ's is the difference between an inquiry and a revelation.

—*Joseph Parker*

WE are perishing for want of wonder, not for want of wonders.

—*Gilbert Keith Chesterton*

MAN is, properly speaking, based upon hope; he has no other possession but hope; this world of his is emphatically the place of hope.

—*Thomas Carlyle*

A blindness to the future! kindly giv'n,
That each may fill the circle mark'd
  by Heav'n;
Who sees with equal eye, as God of all,
A hero perish or a sparrow fall,
Atoms or systems into ruin hurl'd,
And now a bubble burst, and now a
  world.

—*Alexander Pope*

UNBELIEF starves the soul.

—*Richard Cecil*

A mighty fortress is our God,
  A tower of strength ne'er failing.
A helper mighty is our God,
  O'er ills of life prevailing.
He overcometh all.
He saveth from the fall.
  His might and pow'r are great.
  He all things did create,
And he shall reign forever more.

—*Martin Luther*

FAITH is required of thee, and a sincere life.

—*Thomas á Kempis*

THERE is no great future for any people whose faith has burned out.

—*Rufus Jones*

EVERY motion of the constantly shifting bodies in the world, is timed to the occasion for some definite, foreordered end. The flowers blossom in obedience to the same law that marks the course of constellations . . . Nature is one, and to me the greatest delight of observation and study is to discover new unities in this all-embracing and eternal harmony. . . . Men, with only a book of knowledge . . . have seized upon evolution as an escape from the idea of a GOD. 'Evolution!' — a wonderful, mouth-filling word . . . Just say 'evolution' and you have explained every phenomenon of Nature, and explained away GOD. It sounds big and wise. Evolution, they say, brought the earth through its glacial periods, caused the snow blanket to recede, and the flower carpet to follow it, raised the forests of the world, developed animal life from the jelly-fish to the thinking man. But what caused evolution? There they stick. To my mind, it is inconceivable that a plan that has worked out . . . the development of beauty, that has made every microscopic particle of matter perform its function in harmony with every other in the universe — that such a plan is the blind product of an unthinking abstraction. No; somewhere, before evolution was, was an Intelligence . . . You may call that Intelligence what you please; I cannot see why so many people object to call it GOD.

—John Muir

THE Lord is my shepherd; I shall not want.
He maketh me to lie down in green pastures: He leadeth me
    beside the still waters.
He restoreth my soul. He leadeth me in the paths of righteousness
    for his name's sake.
Yea, though I walk through the valley of the shadow of death,
    I will fear no evil: for thou art with me; thy rod and thy
    staff they comfort me.
Thou preparest a table before me in the presence of mine enemies:
    thou anointest my head with oil: my cup runneth over.
Surely goodness and mercy shall follow me all the days of my life:
    and I will dwell in the house of the Lord for ever.

——Old Testament, Psalm 23

DEAR Lord! Kind Lord! Gracious Lord! I pray,
Thou wilt look on all I love, Tenderly today!
Weed their hearts of weariness, Scatter every care
Down a wake of Angel wings
Winnowing the air.

Bring unto the sorrowing All release from pain,
Let the lips of laughter Overflow again;
And with all the needy, O divide, I pray,
This vast treasure of content,
That is mine today.

—James Whitcomb Riley

ALWAYS again there is another day. Always, eternally, there is hope and faith — and tomorrow morning.

—Richard L. Evans

HAPPY is that people . . . whose God is the Lord.

—Old Testament, Psalm 144:15

ALL that I have ever taught of art, everything that I have written, whatever greatness there has been in any thought of mine, whatever I have done in my life, has simply been due to the fact that, when I was a child, my mother daily read with me a part of the Bible, and daily made me learn a part of it by heart.

—John Ruskin

IT is a belief in the Bible . . . which has served me as the guide of my moral and literary life.

—Johann Wolfgang van Goethe

GOD is our refuge and strength, a very present help in trouble.

Therefore will not we fear, though the earth be removed, and though the mountains be carried into the midst of the sea;

Though the waters thereof roar and be troubled, though the mountains shake with the swelling thereof. . . .

He maketh wars to cease unto the end of the earth; he breaketh the bow, and cutteth the spear in sunder; he burneth the chariot in the fire.

Be still, and know that I am God:

—Old Testament, Psalm 46

I thoroughly believe in a university education . . . but I believe a knowledge of the Bible without a college course is more valuable than a college course without the Bible. Everyone who has a thorough knowledge of the Bible may truly be called educated.

—William Lyon Phelps

THERE is no brotherhood of man without the fatherhood of God.

—*Henry Martyn Field*

ERE you left your room this morning, did you think to pray? In the name of Christ, our Savior, did you sue for loving favor as a shield today?

When your heart was filled with anger, did you think to pray? Did you plead for grace, my brother, that you might forgive another who had crossed your way?

When sore trials came upon you, did you think to pray? When your soul was full of sorrow, Balm of Gilead, did you borrow, at the gates of day?

Oh, how praying rests the weary! Prayer will change the night to day; so when life gets dark and dreary, don't forget to pray.

—*Mrs. M. A. Kidder*

THE fool hath said: There is no God!
No God! Who lights the morning sun,
And sends him on his heavenly road,
A far and brilliant course to run?

—*William Knox*

THOSE people who are not governed by God will be ruled by Tyrants.

—*William Penn*

AN atheist is a man who has no visible means of support.

—*Bishop Fulton J. Sheen*

BEHIND everything stands God. . . . Do not avoid, but seek, the great, deep, simple things of faith.

—*Phillips Brooks*

ABIDE with me! fast falls the eventide;
The darkness deepens. Lord, with me abide!
When other helpers fail and comforts flee,
Help of the helpless, O abide with me!

Swift to its close ebbs out life's little day;
Earth's joys grow dim; its glories pass away;
Change and decay in all around I see;
O thou, who changest not, abide with me!

I need thy presence every passing hour;
What but thy grace can foil the tempter's power?
Who like thyself, my guide and stay can be?
Through cloud and sunshine, Lord, abide with me!

—*Henry F. Lyte*

CERTAIN thoughts are prayers. There are moments when, whatever the attitude of the body, the soul is on its knees.

—*Victor Hugo*

I would not lift my little finger to defend the western world against communism if I thought that man were just a machine with no spark of divinity in him.

—*Dwight D. Eisenhower*

I think when I read that sweet story of old,
When Jesus was here among men,
How he called little children like lambs to his fold:
I should like to have been with him then.

I wish that his hands had been placed on my head,
That his arms had been thrown around me,
That I might have seen his kind look when he said,
Let the little ones come unto me.

Yet still to my footstool in prayer I may go,
And ask for a share in his love;
And if I thus earnestly seek him below,
I shall see him and hear Him above.

—Jemima Luke

GOD reveals Himself unfailingly to the thoughtful seeker.

—Honoré de Balzac

VERILY, verily, I say unto you, ye must watch and pray always, . . . Pray in your families unto the Father, always in my name, that your wives and your children may be blessed.

—Book of Mormon
III Nephi 18:15, 21

IF God had commanded me to do all things I could do them.

—Book of Mormon, I Nephi 17:50

WE believe in God, the Eternal Father, and in His Son, Jesus Christ, and in the Holy Ghost.

—Joseph Smith

PRAYER keeps a man from sin, and sin keeps a man from prayer.

—Brigham Young

WHATEVER achievement of my life there is to be commended, the credit is due to my kind parents in instilling into my mind an early love of the Scriptures.

—Daniel Webster

THE earth rolls upon her wings, and the sun giveth his light by day, and the moon giveth her light by night, and the stars also give their light, as they roll upon their wings in their glory, in the midst of the power of God. . . . Behold, all these are kingdoms, and any man who hath seen any or the least of these hath seen God moving in his majesty and power.

—Doctrine & Covenants 88:45-47

UNTIL man has found God, and has been found by God, he begins at no beginning and works to no end. Nothing in the universe or in man's life falls into place except with God.

—H. G. Wells

O my Father, thou that dwellest,
  In the high and glorious place,
When shall I regain thy presence,
  And again behold thy face?
In thy holy habitation,
  Did my spirit once reside?
In my first primeval childhood,
  Was I nurtured near thy side?

For a wise and glorious purpose
  Thou hast placed me here on earth,
And withheld the recollection
  Of my former friends and birth;
Yet ofttimes a secret something
  Whispered, "You're a stranger here,"
And I felt that I had wandered
  From a more exalted sphere.

I had learned to call thee Father,
  Through thy Spirit from on high;
But until the key of knowledge
  Was restored, I knew not why.
In the heavens are parents single?
  No; the thought makes reason stare!
Truth is reason, truth eternal
  Tells me I've a mother there.

When I leave this frail existence,
  When I lay this mortal by,
Father, Mother, may I meet you
  In your royal courts on high?
Then, at length, when I've completed
  All you sent me forth to do,
With your mutual approbation
  Let me come and dwell with you.

—*Eliza R. Snow*

EYE hath not seen, nor ear heard,
neither have entered into the heart
of man, the things which God hath
prepared for them that love him.

—*New Testament, I Corinthians 2:9*

WE act in faith, and miracles occur.

—*Dag Hammerskjold*

I know not by what method rare,
But this I know, God answers prayer.
I know that He has given His word,
That tells me prayer is always heard,
And will be answered, soon or late,
And so I pray and calmly wait.
I know not if the blessing sought,
Will come just in the way I thought,
But leave my prayers with Him above,
Whose ways are wiser than my own,
Assured that He will grant my quest
Or send some answer far more blessed.

—*Author Unknown*

WHEN thou liest down, thou shalt
not be afraid . . . and thy sleep shall
be sweet.

—*Old Testament, Proverbs 3:24*

OUR Father which art in heaven,
Hallowed be thy name.
Thy kingdom come.
Thy will be done
  in earth, as it is in heaven.

Give us this day
  our daily bread.
And forgive us our debts,
  as we forgive our debtors.
And lead us not into temptation,
  but deliver us from evil:

For thine is the kingdom,
  and the power,
  and the glory,
  forever. Amen.

—*New Testament, Matthew 6:9-13*

GOD is greater than your greatest need.

—*C. Mervyn Maxwell*

THE future is no more uncertain than the present.

—*Walt Whitman*

SURELY the Lord God will do nothing, but he revealeth his secret unto his servants the prophets.

—*Old Testament, Amos 3:7*

WHERE there is no vision, the people perish.

—*Old Testament, Proverbs 29:18*

WE believe all that God has revealed, all that He does now reveal, and we believe He will yet reveal many great and important things pertaining to the Kingdom of God.

—*Joseph Smith*

HAVE courage for the great sorrows of life, and patience for the small ones; and when you have laboriously accomplished your daily task, go to sleep in peace. God is awake.

—*Victor Hugo*

IT has taken me all my life to understand that it is not necessary to understand everything.

—*Author Unknown*

I am a child of God,
And He has sent me here,
Has given me an earthly home
With parents kind and dear.

Lead me, guide me, walk beside me,
Help me find the way.
Teach me all that I must do
To live with Him some day.

—*Naomi W. Randall*

Part 10

Happiness, Peace; Sorrow, Discouragement

Endure, and keep yourselves for days of happiness.

—Virgil

LIFE is too short for mean anxieties.

—*Charles Kingsley*

ONE who expects completely to escape low moods is asking the impossible. . . . Like the weather, life is essentially variable, . . . and a healthy person believes in the validity of his high hours even when he is having a low one.

—*Harry Emerson Fosdick*

WHILE each of us, . . . has depressed hours, none of us needs to be a depressed person.

—*Henry Emerson Fosdick*

WE degrade life by our follies and vices, and then complain that the unhappiness which is only their accompaniment is inherent in the constitution of things.

—*Christian Nestell Bovee*

SOMEWHERE there waiteth in this world of ours
　　For one lone soul another lonely soul,
Each choosing each through all the weary hours.
　　And meeting strangely at one sudden goal,
Then blend they, like green leaves with golden flowers,
　　Into one beautiful perfect whole;
And life's long night is ended, and the way
　　Lies open onward to eternal day.

—*Sir Edwin Arnold*

I know no occupation in life more barren of results than the permanent seeking of pleasure. Pleasure is a by-product of doing something that is worth doing. Therefore, do not seek pleasure as such. Pleasure comes of seeking something else, and comes by the way. The whole point of enjoying recreation is that it is not your permanent occupation. The man who is seeking pleasure as his main occupation in life never has any recreation because he never can turn to anything else.

—A. Lawrence Lowell

THE grand essentials to happiness in this life are something to do, something to love, and something to hope for.

—Joseph Addison

THE thing that counts most in the pursuit of happiness is choosing the right traveling companion.

—Adrian Anderson

THE supreme happiness of life is the conviction that we are loved.

—Victor Hugo

WE all have strength enough to bear the misfortunes of others.

—La Rochefoucauld

PEACE be both to thee, and peace be to thine house, and peace be unto all that thou hast.

—Old Testament, I Samuel 25:6

ALL who joy would win must share it. Happiness was born a twin.

—Lord Byron

I have observed a number of superficially contented men and women, and I maintain they are dangerous. Personally, I am glad to say there are a lot of things today with which I am not contented. I am not contented with myself, with the development of my character, and with my literary career. And there seems to me very little ground for general contentment. I must repeat — I fear the contented man. I fear him because there is no progress unless there is discontent. Without it today, I even believe, there can be no inner peace of mind.

—John P. Marquand

BLESSED are the peace-makers: for they shall be called the children of God.

—New Testament, Matthew 5:9

AND the peace of God, which passeth all understanding, shall keep your hearts and minds through Christ Jesus.

—New Testament, Philippians 4:7

THE end of war is peace.

—Cervantes

1. Sit quietly for a moment, and you realize how you have been foolishly running about.
2. Learn to keep your mouth shut, and you realize you have been talking too much.
3. Avoid getting involved in too many things, and you realize that you have been wasting your time in unnecessary things.
4. Close your door, and you realize that you have been mixed up with too many kinds of people.
5. Have few desires, and you realize why you have had so many ills.
6. Be human, and you realize that you have been too critical of others.

—Chen Chiju (1588-1639)

LET us therefore follow after the things which make for peace.

—New Testament, Romans 14:19

I have lived to know that the great secret of human happiness is this: never suffer your energies to stagnate.

—Adam Clarke

WHO walks a road with love will never walk that road alone again.

—Charles Thomas Davis

THE height of human wisdom is to bring our tempers down to our circumstances — and to make a calm within, under the weight of the greatest storm without.

—Daniel Defoe

THE devil . . . seeketh that all men might be miserable like unto himself.

Book of Mormon, II Nephi 2:27

IT is necessary to the happiness of man that he be mentally faithful to himself.

—Thomas Paine

EVERY man has his secret sorrows which the world knows not; and oftentimes we call a man cold when he is only sad.

—Henry Wadsworth Longfellow

THERE is an evident effort in nature to be happy. Everything blossoms to express beauty, as well as lead to fruitage. Even the inorganic fashions itself into crystals, that absorb and flash back the sunlight. . . . If one examines nature with the microscope . . . or considers the heavens at night, he finds three things: truth as inherent, beauty beyond that which can be spoken, and goodness everywhere. . . . God speaks through all things, with an eternal desire to create happiness. Man has no right to be an exception — the only pessimist in the universe. The deep distress of the world comes in when we lose our anchorage of faith in Him.

—Editorial: The Outlook

FIRST keep thyself in peace, and then shalt thou be able to be a peacemaker towards others. A peaceable man doth more good than a well-learned. A passionate man turneth even good into evil and easily believeth evil; a good, peaceable man converteth all things into good. He who dwelleth in peace is suspicious of none, but he who is discontented and restless is tossed with many suspicions, and is neither quiet himself nor suffereth others to be quiet. He often saith what he ought not to say, and omitteth what it were more expedient for him to do. He considereth to what duties others are bound, and neglecteth those to which he is bound himself. Therefore be zealous first over thyself, and then mayest thou righteously be zealous concerning thy neighbour. . . . There are those who keep themselves in peace and keep peace also with others, and there are those who neither have peace nor suffer others to have peace; they are troublesome to others, but always more troublesome to themselves. And there are those who hold themselves in peace, and study to bring others unto peace; nevertheless, all our peace in this sad life lieth in humble suffering rather than in not feeling adversities. He who best knoweth how to suffer shall possess the most peace; that man is conqueror of himself and Lord of the world, the friend of Christ, and the inheritor of heaven.

—Thomas á Kempis

IT is necessary to hope, . . . for hope itself is happiness.

—Samuel Johnson

HE who doeth the works of righteousness shall receive his reward, even peace in this world, and eternal life in the world to come.

—Doctrine & Covenants 59:23

THE whole life of man is but a point of time; let us enjoy it, therefore, while it lasts, and not spend it to no purpose.

—Plutarch

SO long as man is alive and free, he will, in one way or another, seek that which gives him pleasure. But . . . to seek is not necessarily to find. . . . The basis of happiness is abundance of life, and abundance of life is a real thing, that cannot be shammed or counterfeited.

—David Starr Jordan

LITTLE do men perceive what solitude is, and how far it extendeth, for a crowd is not company, and faces are but a gallery of pictures, and talk but a tinkling cymbal where there is no love.

—Sir John Lubbock

IN vain do they talk of happiness who never subdued an impulse in obedience to a principle. He who never sacrificed a present to a future good, or a personal to a general one, can speak of happiness only as the blind do of colors.

—*Horace Mann*

OUR goal must be — not peace in our time — but peace for all time.

—*Harry S. Truman*

HEED how thou livest. Do not act by day
Which from the night shall drive thy peace away.

—*John Greenleaf Whittier*

STAY, stay at home, my heart and rest;
Home-keeping hearts are happiest,
For those that wander they know not where
Are full of trouble and full of care;
    To stay at home is best.

Weary and homesick and distressed,
They wander east, they wander west,
And are baffled and beaten and blown about
By the winds of the wilderness of doubt;
    To stay at home is best.

Then stay at home, my heart, and rest;
The bird is safest in its nest,
Over all that flutter their wings and fly
A hawk is hovering in the sky;
    To stay at home is best.

—*Henry Wadsworth Longfellow*

PEOPLE are lonely because they build walls instead of bridges.

—*Joseph Fort Newton*

NO longer forward nor behind
    I look in hope or fear;
But grateful, take the good I find,
    The best of now and here.

—*John Greenleaf Whittier*

ON morning wings how active springs the mind
That leaves the load of yesterday behind!

—*Alexander Pope*

YOU may satisfy all your senses and still not be satisfied.

—*Edward S. Martin*

HAPPINESS makes up in height for what it lacks in length.

—*Robert Frost*

THERE are three means of achieving the happy, abundant life: first, making God the center of one's life; second, using the free agency given to man; and third, rendering service to others.

—*David O. McKay*

OH, make us happy and you make us good.

—*Robert Browning*

I have had many troubles in my life, but the worst of them never came.

—*James A. Garfield*

THERE is no peace on earth today
Save the peace in the heart at home
with God. . . .
No man can be at peace with his
neighbor who is not at peace with
himself.

—*Edna St. Vincent Millay*

HAPPINESS is the object and design of our existence; and will be the end thereof, if we pursue the path that leads to it; and this path is virtue, uprightness, faithfulness, holiness, and keeping all the commandments of God.

—*Joseph Smith*

EVILS have their life, their limits.

—*Montaigne*

IF all men were to bring their miseries together in one place, most would be glad to take each his own home again rather than take a portion out of the common stock.

—*Solon*

WE can easily manage, if we will only take each day, the burden appointed for it. But the load will be too heavy for us if we carry yesterday's burden over again today, and then add the burden of the morrow to the weight before we are required to bear it.

—*John Newton*

IT is wrong to sorrow without ceasing.

—*Homer*

IF one only wished to be happy, this could be easily accomplished; but we wish to be happier than other people, and this is always difficult, for we believe others to be happier than they are.

—*Montesquieu*

THERE is no loneliness so great, so absolute, so utterly complete, as the loneliness of a man who cannot call upon his God.

—*Richard L. Evans*

REASON and sense remove anxiety,
Not houses that look out upon the sea.
Why should we move to find countries
and climates of another kind?
What exile leaves himself behind?

—*Horace*

WE have no more right to consume happiness without producing it than to consume wealth without producing it.

—*George Bernard Shaw*

THE soul that perpetually overflows with kindness and sympathy will always be cheerful.

—*Parke Godwin*

I am more and more convinced that our happiness depends far more on the way we meet the events of life than on the nature of those events themselves.

—*Frederich H. Humboldt*

WE can't choose happiness either for ourselves or for another; we can't tell where that will lie. We can only choose whether we will indulge ourselves in the present moment, or whether we will renounce that, for the sake of obeying the Divine Voice within us, — for the sake of being true to all the motives that sanctify our lives.

—*George Eliot*

I know what happiness is, for I have done good work.

—*Robert Louis Stevenson*

I came at morn; 'twas spring, I smiled,
The fields with green were clad;
I walked abroad at noon, and lo!
'Twas summer — I was glad;
I sate me down; 'twas autumn eve,
And I with sadness wept;
I laid me down at night, and then
'Twas winter, and I slept.

—*Mary Pyper*

A light heart lives long.

—*Shakespeare*

THERE is no duty we so much underrate as the duty of being happy.

—*Robert Louis Stevenson*

IT is indeed foolish to be unhappy now because you may be unhappy at some future time.

—*Seneca*

WHATEVER hour God has blessed you with, take it with grateful hand, nor postpone your joys from year to year, so that, in whatever place you have been, you may say that you have lived happily.

—*Horace*

MANY run about after happiness like an absent-minded man hunting for his hat, while it is in his hand or on his head.

—*James Sharp*

A merry heart doeth good like a medicine: but a broken spirit drieth the bones.

—*Old Testament, Proverbs 17:22*

GRIEF can take care of itself; but to get the full value of joy, you must have somebody to share it with.

—*Mark Twain*

ANY pleasure which keeps the heart from God will be fatal to the soul.

—*Richard Fuller*

PEACE is such a precious jewel that I would give anything for it but truth.

—*Matthew Henry*

A good laugh is sunshine in a house.

—*William Makepeace Thackeray*

THOSE who are at war with others are not at peace with themselves.

—*William Hazlitt*

NOTHING can bring you peace but yourself; nothing can bring you peace but the triumph of principles.

—*Ralph Waldo Emerson*

HIM only pleasure leads, and peace attends,
Whose means are fair and spotless as his ends.

—*William Wordsworth*

IF we have not peace within ourselves, it is in vain to seek it from outward sources.

—*Author Unknown*

I had a pleasant time with my mind, for it was happy.

—*Louisa May Alcott*

THE secret of happiness is not in doing what one likes to do, but in liking what one has to do.

—*Sir James M. Barrie*

GLADNESS of the heart is the life of man, and the joyfulness of a man prolongeth his days.

—*Ecclesiasticus 30:22 (Apocrypha)*

NOW beautiful upon the mountains are the feet of him that bringeth good tidings, that publisheth peace; . . . that saith unto Zion, Thy God reigneth!

—*Old Testament, Isaiah 52:7*

TO understand and to be understood makes our happiness on earth.

—*German Proverb*

SORROW is a disease in which every patient must treat himself.

—*Voltaire*

MEN are that they might have joy.

—*Book of Mormon, II Nephi 2:25*

WHEN upon life's billows you are tempest-tossed,

When you are discouraged, thinking all is lost,

Count your many blessings; name them one by one,

And it will surprise you what the Lord has done.

Are you ever burdened with a load of care?

Does the cross seem heavy you are called to bear?

Count your many blessings; every doubt will fly,

And you will be singing as the days go by.

When you look at others with their lands and gold,

Think that Christ has promised you his wealth untold.

Count your many blessings; money cannot buy

Your reward in heaven nor your home on high.

So amid the conflict, whether great or small,

Do not be discouraged; God is over all.

Count your many blessings; angels will attend,

Help and comfort give you to your journey's end.

—J. Oatman, Jr.

JOY is not in things; it is in us.

—*Richard Wagner*

WHATEVER comes, this too shall pass away.

—*Ella Wheeler Wilcox*

DESPONDENCY is the most unprofitable feeling a man can indulge in.

—*DeWitt Talmage*

HAPPINESS is not a station you arrive at, but a manner of traveling.

—*Margaret Lee Runbeck*

Part II

Attitudes:
Anger, Courage, Fear; Honesty, Humility, Patience, Pride

The world is too narrow for two fools a quarrelling.

—THOMAS FULLER

MY life is in the hands of any fool who makes me lose my temper.

—Dr. John Hunter

THESE six things doth the Lord hate: yea, seven are an abomination unto him: A proud look, a lying tongue, and hands that shed innocent blood, An heart that deviseth wicked imaginations, feet that be swift in running to mischief, A false witness that speaketh lies, and he that soweth discord among brethren.

—Old Testament, Proverbs 6:16-19

NO man has a good enough memory to be a successful liar.

—Abraham Lincoln

THE most exhausting thing in life is being insincere.

—Anne Morrow Lindbergh

THE heart has its arguments with which the logic of the mind is not acquainted.

—Blaise Pascal

IF we would only testify to the truth as we see it, it would turn out at once that there are hundreds, thousands, and even millions of men just as we are, who see the truth as we do, are afraid as we are of seeming to be singular by confessing it, and are only waiting, again as we are, for someone to proclaim it.

—Leo Tolstoi

THE end of anger is sorrow.

—Seneca

THE worst-tempered people I've ever met were those people who knew they were wrong.

—Wilson Mizner

NGER is the most dangerous of all passions; — the most unmannerly; — Reason deliberates before it judges; — but anger passes sentence without deliberation; . . . it leaves no place for counsel, or friendship, honesty, or good manners; . . . it falls many times upon the wrong person; upon the innocent, [and] tears all to pieces. It is most certain that we might govern our anger, if we would; for the same thing that [angers] us at home, gives us no offense at all abroad; and what is the reason? We are patient in one place, and [not] in another.

—Seneca

HE greatest remedy for anger is delay.

—Seneca

WHEN angry, count ten before you speak, if very angry, count a hundred.

—Thomas Jefferson

A soft answer turneth away wrath: but grievous words stir up anger.

—Old Testament, Proverbs 15:1

WHEN a man is wrong and won't admit it, he always gets angry.

—Thomas Chandler Haliburton

TO see what is right and not to do it, is want of courage.

—Confucius

CONSIDER, when you are enraged at any one, what you would probably think if he should die during the dispute.

—William Shenstone

NO mind is thoroughly well organized that is deficient in a sense of humor.

—Samuel Taylor Coleridge

FREQUENT fits of anger produce in the soul a propensity to be angry; which ofttimes ends in choler, bitterness, and morosity, when the mind becomes ulcerated, peevish, and querulous, and is wounded by the least occurrence.

—Plutarch

LITTLE by little, through patience and longsuffering, thou shalt conquer by the help of God.

—Thomas á Kempis

ACT nothing in a furious passion. It is putting to sea in a storm.

—Thomas Fuller

WHEN anger rises, think of the consequences.

—Confucius

I'LL not willingly offend,
  Nor be easily offended:
What's amiss I'll strive to mend,
  And endure what can't be mended.

—*Isaac Watts*

TO be in a passion you good may do,
But no good if a passion is in you.

—*William Blake*

HE who fears loses strength for the combat of life, for the fight against evil.

—*John A. Widtsoe*

MEN often make up in wrath what they want in reason.

—*William R. Alger*

ANGER may repast with thee for an hour, but not repose for a night; the continuance of anger is hatred, the continuance of hatred turns malice. That anger is not warrantable which hath seen two suns.

—*Francis Quarles*

TO be sincere with ourselves is better and harder than to be painstakingly accurate with others.

—*Agnes Repplier*

GIVE not reins to your inflamed passions; take time and a little delay; impetuosity manages all things badly.

—*Statius*

WHATEVER the situation, . . . and however . . . disheartening it may be, it is a great hour when a man ceases adopting [difficulties] as an excuse for despondency and tackles himself as the real problem. No mood need be his master. . . . Remember others. Emotions are contagious . . . [and] can infect a whole household.

—*Harry Emerson Fosdick*

PATIENCE is the support of weakness; impatience is the ruin of strength.

—*Charles Caleb Colton*

HE who is conscious of secret and dark designs which, if known, would blast him, is perpetually shrinking and dodging from public observation, and is afraid of all around and much more of all above him.

—*William Wirt*

LIFE appears to me too short to be spent in nursing animosity or registering wrong.

—*Charlotte Bronte*

TRUE courage is not the brutal force of vulgar heroes, but the firm resolve of virtue and reason.

—*Paul Whitehead*

AN angry man stirreth up strife, and a furious man aboundeth in transgression.

—*Old Testament, Proverbs 29:22*

ANYBODY can become angry —
— that is easy; but to be angry with
the right person, and to the right degree, and at the right time, and for
the right purpose, and in the right way
— that is not within everybody's
power and is not easy.

—*Aristotle*

PASSION is a sort of fever in the
mind, which ever leaves us weaker
than it found us.

—*William Penn*

PEOPLE are always talking of perseverance, and courage and fortitude;
but patience is the finest and worthiest
part of fortitude, and the rarest, too.

—*John Ruskin*

WE are what we are, wherever we
are.

—*Richard L. Evans*

ANGER, if not restrained, is frequently more hurtful to us than the
injury that provokes it.

—*Seneca*

HE who can suppress a moment's
anger may prevent a day of sorrow.

—*Tryon Edwards*

THERE is not in nature a thing
that makes man so deformed, so
beastly, as doth intemperate anger.

—*John Webster*

HUMAN vanity can best be served
by a reminder that, whatever his
accomplishments, his sophistication,
his artistic pretention, man owes his
very existence to a six-inch layer of
top soil — and the fact that it rains.

—*Author Unknown*

THE thing I most pity in men is —
action prompted by surprise of anger.

—*Robert Browning*

WHEN thou art above measure
angry, bethink thee how momentary is
man's life.

—*Marcus Aurelius*

LOSS of sincerity is loss of vital
power.

—*Christian Nestell Bovee*

HE that corrects out of passion,
raises revenge sooner than repentance.

—*William Penn*

HOW poor are they who have not
patience! What wound did ever heal
but by degrees?

—*Shakespeare*

IT'S easy finding reasons why other
folks should be patient.

—*George Eliot*

HE is a fool who cannot be angry;
but he is a wise man who will not.

—*Old Saying*

NO man is himself in acute sorrow. No man is himself in anger. No man is himself with feelings of offense. And decisions that will wait are safer with waiting — waiting for time to take over, for the dust to clear away, for tempers to cool, for perspective to return, for the real issues to show themselves, for the real values to reappear, for judgment to emerge and mature.

We should think seriously before we slam doors, before we burn bridges, before we saw off the limb on which we find ourselves sitting. Decisions in acute sorrow, decisions in anger, decisions under pressure, decisions that haven't been thought through are less likely to be mature and safe decisions.

—Richard L. Evans

COURAGE is the greatest of all the virtues, because if you haven't courage, you may not have an opportunity to use any of the others.

—Samuel Johnson

WITHOUT humility there can be no humanity.

—Sir John Buchan

BE patient in little things. Learn to meet the everyday trials and annoyances of life quietly and calmly, and then, when unforeseen trouble or calamity comes, your strength will not forsake you.

—William Plumer

BE not hasty in thy spirit to be angry, for anger resteth in the bosom of fools.

—Old Testament, Ecclesiastes 7:9

OFTEN the test of courage is not to die but to live.

—Vittorio Alfieri

IT is impossible to indulge in habitual severity of opinion upon our fellow-men without injuring the tenderness and delicacy of our own feelings.

—Henry Ward Beecher

LORD, make me humble, but don't let me know it!

—Dwight L. Moody

WE must learn not to let the fear of failure make us fail, and not to let our fears make our failures final.

—Richard L. Evans

THERE is none so great but he may both need the help and service . . . even of the meanest of mortals.

—Seneca

HUMILITY is the ability *to act* embarrassed when you tell people how wonderful you are.

—S. Lee Luchansky

PROFOUND sincerity is the only basis of talent, as of character.

—*Ralph Waldo Emerson*

GOD has made no one absolute. . . . No one subsists by himself alone.

—*Owen Feltham*

LET every man be swift to hear, slow to speak, slow to wrath.

—*New Testament, James 1:19*

AN angry man is again angry with himself when he returns to reason.

—*Publius Syrus*

CONSIDER how much more you often suffer from your anger and grief than from those very things for which you are angry and grieved.

—*Marcus Aurelius*

NEVER trust your tongue when your heart is bitter.

—*Samuel J. Hurwitt*

HE that would be angry and sin not, must not be angry with anything but sin.

—*Thomas Secker*

HE that saith he is in the light, and hateth his brother, is in darkness.

—*New Testament, I John 2:9*

WITHOUT fear there are no heroes, only fools. Never stop being afraid.

—*Author Unknown*

THE greatest and sublimest power is often simple patience.

—*Horace Bushnell*

PASSION is the drunkenness of the mind.

—*Robert South*

PASSION costs me too much to bestow it on every trifle.

—*Thomas Adams*

FEAR of misfortune is worse than misfortune itself.

—*Najile S. Khoury*

WHAT a new face courage puts on everything!

—*Ralph Waldo Emerson*

THE honest man must keep faith with himself; his sheer anchor is sincerity.

—*Ralph Waldo Emerson*

HYPOCRISY is folly. It is much easier, safer, and pleasanter to be the thing which a man appears, than to keep up the appearance of what he is not.

—*Richard Cecil*

ANGER begins in folly, and ends in repentance.

—*Pythagoras*

TO be honest, to be kind;
To earn a little and to spend a little less;
To make upon the whole a family happier for his presence;
To renounce when that shall be necessary and not to be embittered;
To keep a few friends, but those without capitulation, —
Above all, on the same grim conditions, to keep friends with
    himself—
Here is a task for all that a man has of fortitude and delicacy.

—*Robert Louis Stevenson*

THE greatest discovery of my generation is that human beings can alter their lives by altering their attitudes of mind.

—*William James*

THE future into which you walk is as dark to you as the pavement before the feet of the blind. When next you see a blind man walking down a busy street, do not think to yourself, "There goes an unusual man!" The courage to walk into the unknown is the courage required of all human beings. Think instead, "There goes a man who knows no more about his next step than I do about mine. In this world we are all brothers."

—*Robert Russell*

THE lofty looks of man shall be humbled, and the haughtiness of men shall be bowed down.

—*Old Testament, Isiah 2:11*

WHEN a mouse falls into a meal sack, he thinks he is the miller himself.

—*Dutch Proverb*

NOT to be provok'd is best: But if mov'd never correct till the Fume is spent;
For every stroke our fury strikes, is sure to hit ourselves at last.

—*William Penn*

PEOPLE who think they are too big to do little things are perhaps too little to be asked to do big things.

—*Author Unknown*

PRIDE goeth before destruction, and an haughty spirit before a fall.

—*Old Testament, Proverbs 16:18*

IT is easy to entertain egoists — just sit and listen.

—*Author Unknown*

LOOK not mournfully into the Past. It comes not back again. Wisely improve the Present. It is thine. Go forth to meet the shadowy Future, without fear, and with a manly heart.

—*Henry Wadsworth Longfellow*

IT is only when you don't run from yourself that you begin to get somewhere.

—*Author Unknown*

I have been more and more convinced the more I think of it that in general pride is at the bottom of all great mistakes.

—*John Ruskin*

BE yourself if you ever hope to be somebody.

—*Author Unknown*

SNOBBERY is the pride of those who are not sure of their positions.

—*Author Unknown*

KEEP cool and you command everybody.

—*Louis Léon de Saint-Just*

LET not the sun go down upon your wrath.

—*New Testament, Ephesians 4:26*

LIFE is a long lesson in humility.

—*Sir James M. Barrie*

Part 12

Getting Along with People: Friendship, Trust, Kindness, Good Manners, and Understanding Others

Perhaps any of us could get along with perfect people. But our task is to get along with imperfect people.

—Richard L. Evans

THE greatest sin against mankind is not to hate them — but to be indifferent to them.

—*George Bernard Shaw*

JULIA Ward Howe was talking to a distinguished senator. She asked him to interest himself in the case of a person who needed help. The senator answered, "Julia, I have become so busy, I can no longer concern myself with individuals." She replied, "That's remarkable. Even God hasn't reached that stage yet."

—*Ralph W. Sockman*

I have taken my best pains not to laugh at the actions of mankind, not to groan over them, not to be angry with them, but to understand them.

—*Baurch Spinoza*

LIFE is not so short but there is always time enough for courtesy.

—*Ralph Waldo Emerson*

THERE is nothing so strong as gentleness, and there is nothing so gentle as real strength.

—*St. Francis de Sales*

OH, the comfort, the inexpressible comfort, of feeling safe with a person, having neither to weigh thoughts, nor measure words — but pouring them all right out — just as they are — chaff and grain together — certain that a faithful hand will take and sift them — keep what is worth keeping — and with the breath of kindness blow the rest away.

—*Dinah Maria Mulock*

THEREFORE all things whatsoever ye would that men should do to you, do ye even so to them: for this is the law and the prophets.

—*New Testament, Matthew 7:12*

IN most quarrels there is a fault on both sides. A quarrel may be compared to a spark, which cannot be produced without a flint as well as steel.

—*Charles Caleb Colton*

KINDNESS is produced by kindness.

—*Cicero*

THREE-FOURTHS of the people you will meet tomorrow are hungering and thirsting for sympathy. Give it to them, and they will love you.

—*Dale Carnegie*

I am a man, and nothing that concerns a man do I deem a matter of indifference to me.

—*Terence*

A new commandment I give unto you, That ye love one another; as I have loved you, that ye also love one another.

—*New Testament, John 13:34*

I know nothing which life has to offer so satisfying as the profound good understanding . . . between two virtuous men, each of whom is sure of himself, and sure of his friend.

—*Ralph Waldo Emerson*

ALL doors are open to courtesy.

—*Thomas Fuller*

SELF-RESPECT is at the bottom of all good manners. They are the expression of discipline, of good-will, of respect for other people's rights and comfort and feelings.

—*Edward S. Martin*

RESPECT a man, he will do the more.

—*James Howell*

YEARS ago I preferred clever people. There was a joy in beholding . . . a mind . . . bearing thoughts quickly translated into words, or ideas expressed in a new way. I find now that my taste has changed. Verbal fireworks often bore me. They seem motivated by self-assertion and self-display. I now prefer another type of person; one who is considerate, understanding of others, careful not to break down another person's self-respect. . . . My preferred person today is one who is always aware of the needs of others, or their pain and fear and unhappiness, and their search for self-respect. . . . I once liked clever people. Now I like good people.

—*Solomon Bennett Freehof*

THERE'S a destiny that makes us
brothers.
None goes his way alone.
All that we send into the lives of
others,
Will come back into our own.

—*Edwin Markham*

FRICTION does not have to be
screechy . . . to be dangerous and
evil. [It] can trigger chain reactions
and shake the whole delicate balance
of office or workshop or home [or of
the whole world].

—*The Royal Bank of Canada
Monthly Letter*

YOU are surrounded by hundreds
of people more timid than you are.

—*Fred S. Barton*

REPROVE thy friend privately;
commend him publicly.

—*Old Saying*

GREAT God of all the earth,
Lead us to know the worth
Of sympathy;
May fellowship increase,
May all contention cease,
O may we dwell in peace
And unity.

—*Leonard B. McWhood
Hymn of Nations*

THE deepest urge in human nature
is the desire to be important.

—*John Dewey*

BE polite, prepare yourself for
whatever you are asked to do, keep
yourself tidy, be cheerful, don't be
envious, be honest with yourself so
you will be honest with others, be
helpful, interest yourself in your job,
don't pity yourself, be quick to praise,
be loyal to your friends, avoid prejudices, be independent . . . and read
the newspapers.

—*Bernard Baruch*

AS laws are necessary that good
manners may be preserved, so good
manners are necessary that laws may
be maintained.

—*Niccolo Machiavelli*

I have wept in the night
For the shortness of sight
That to somebody's need made me
blind;
But I never have yet
Felt a tinge of regret
For being a little too kind.

—*Author Unknown*

IF we lose affection and kindliness
from our life, we lose all that gives
it charm.

—*Cicero*

BEAR ye one another's burdens,
and so fulfill the law of Christ.

—*New Testament, Galatians 6:2*

HE who would find a friend without faults will be without friends.

—*Author Unknown*

THIS is the law of benefits between men: the one ought to forget at once what he has given, and the other ought never to forget what he has received.

—*Seneca*

HE jests at scars that never felt a wound.

—*Shakespeare*

WORDS as hard as cannon-balls . . .

—*Ralph Waldo Emerson*

GOOD Will is the mightiest practical force in the universe.

—*C. F. Dole*

CONFIDENCE is a subtle thing. It is built slowly and can be easily and quickly shaken.

—*George Humphrey*

THE best way to destroy an enemy is to change him into a friend.

—*Author Unknown*

WHEREVER there is a human being there is a chance for a kindness.

—*Seneca*

MEN build too many walls and not enough bridges.

—*Sir Isaac Newton*

LET us oft speak kind words to each other
    At home or where'er we may be;
Like the warblings of birds on the heather,
    The tones will be welcome and free.

They'll gladden the heart that's repining,
    Give courage and hope from above,
And where the dark clouds hide the shining,
    Let in the bright sunlight of love.

Like the sunbeams of morn on the mountains,
    The soul they awake to good cheer;
Like the murmur of cool, pleasant fountains,
    They fall in sweet cadences near.

Let's oft, then, in kindly toned voices,
    Our mutual friendship renew,
Till heart meets with heart and rejoices
    In friendship that ever is true.

Chorus:

O the kind words we give shall in memory live
    And sunshine forever impart;
Let us oft speak kind words to each other;
    Kind words are sweet tones of the heart.

—*Joseph L. Townsend*

TRIFLES, little attentions, mere nothings, either done or neglected, will make you either liked or disliked in the general run of the world.

Lord Chesterfield

THE art of acceptance is the art of making someone who has done you a small favor wish that he might have done you a greater one.

—Russell Lynes

TIME to me this truth has taught,
  ('Tis a treasure worth revealing)
More offend from want of thought
  Than from any want of feeling.

—Charles Swain

IF only I may grow: firmer, simpler, quieter, warmer.

—Dag Hammerskjold

WHERE pity dwells the peace of God is there.

—John Greenleaf Whittier

THE man who trusts men will make fewer mistakes than he who distrusts them.

—Camillo Di Cavour

TO know someone here or there with whom you can feel there is understanding in spite of distances or thoughts unexpressed — that can make of this earth a garden.

—Johann Wolfgang von Goethe

TAKE care. It is so easy to break eggs without making omelettes.

—Clive Staples Lewis

TO be a gentleman is to be one all the world over, and in every relation and grade of society.

—Robert Louis Stevenson

BETTER throw a stone at random than a word.

—Pope Xystus I

THE simple virtues of willingness, readiness, alertness and courtesy will carry a young man farther than mere smartness.

—Henry P. Daveson

FROM quiet homes and first
  beginnings,
Out to the undiscovered ends,
There's nothing worth the wear of
  living,
But laughter and love and friends.

—Author Unknown

MANNERS are of more importance than laws. Upon them in a great measure, the laws depend. The law touches us but here and there, and now and then. Manners are what vex or soothe, corrupt or purify, exalt or debase, barbarize or refine us, by a constant, steady, uniform, insensible operation, like that of the air we breathe.

—Edmund Burke

NOT understood. We move along asunder,
　　Our paths grow wider as the seasons creep
Along the years; we marvel and we wonder
　　Why life is life, and then we fall asleep,
　　　　Not understood.

Not understood. We gather false impressions
　　And hug them closer as the years go by,
Till virtues often seem to us transgressions;
　　And thus men rise and fall and live and die,
　　　　Not understood.

Not understood. Poor souls with stunted vision
　　Oft measure giants by their narrow gauge.
The poisoned shafts of falsehood and derision
　　Are oft impelled 'gainst those who mould the age,
　　　　Not understood.

Not understood. The secret springs of action,
　　Which lie beneath the surface and the show,
Are disregarded; with self-satisfaction
　　We judge our neighbors as they often go,
　　　　Not understood.

Not understood. How trifles often change us.
　　The thoughtless sentence or the fancied slight
Destroys long years of friendships, and estranges us,
　　And on our souls there falls a freezing blight:
　　　　Not understood.

Not understood. How many breasts are aching,
　　For lack of sympathy? Ah! day to day,
How many cheerless, lonely hearts are breaking!
　　How many noble spirits pass away,
　　　　Not understood.

O God, that men would see a little clearer,
　　Or judge less harshly where they cannot see!
O God, that men would draw a little nearer
　　To one another! They'd be nearer Thee
　　　　And understood.

　　　　　　　　　　　—*Thomas Bracken*

To wake the soul by tender strokes of art
To raise the genius, and to mend the heart;
To make mankind, in conscious virtue bold
Live o'er each scene, and be what they behold.

—Alexander Pope

I have yet to find a man, whatever his situation in life, who did not do better work and put forth greater effort under a spirit of approval than he ever would do under a spirit of criticism.

—Charles M. Schwab

THERE can be no friendship without confidence, and no confidence without integrity.

—Samuel Johnson

I used to think of impatience as simply a natural part of some people's personality, but over the years I have come to conclude that habitual impatience is a mark of immaturity.

—Dr. Harold Lee Snow

OF all things which wisdom provides to make life entirely happy, much the greatest is the possession of friendship.

—Epicurus

NO civilization is complete which does not include the dumb and defenseless of God's creatures within the sphere of charity and mercy.

—Queen Victoria

TOLERANCE without compromising truth or principles is one of the great needs of the hour.

—Richard L. Evans

I love humanity — but I can't stand people personally.

—Author Unknown

MAN to man shall brothers be
Throughout the world for a' that.

—Robert Burns

IF a man does not make new acquaintances as he advances through life, he will soon find himself alone. A man, sir, must keep his friendships in constant repair.

—Samuel Johnson

NO one is useless in this world who lightens the burden of it to anyone else.

—Charles Dickens

A smile is a curved line that sets things straight.

—Author Unknown

WE are all fellow passengers on the same planet.

—Hendrick van Loon

THE quality of mercy is not strain'd.
It droppeth as the gentle rain from heaven
Upon the place beneath: it is twice blest:
It blesseth him that gives and him that takes.
'Tis mightiest in the mightiest; it becomes
The throned monarch better than his crown.
His sceptre shows the force of temporal power,
The attribute to awe and majesty,
Wherein doth sit the dread and fear of kings;
It is an attribute to God himself;
And earthly power doth then show likest God's
When mercy seasons justice.

—Shakespeare

AFFECTION can withstand very severe storms of vigor, but not a long polar frost of indifference.

—Sir Walter Scott

IF we want happiness with loved ones, and peace, and quiet conscience, we need to learn the little lessons, the small services, the continuing kindnesses, the habitual acts of honesty, the constancy of cleanliness — not just one big washing.

—Richard L. Evans

IT is not the shilling I give you that counts, but the warmth that it carries with it from my hand.

—Miguel de Unamuno'

HIS life was gentle, and the elements so mixed in him that
Nature might stand up and say to all the world: This was a man.

—Shakespeare

I would rather be in company with a dead man than with an absent one; for if the dead man gives me no pleasure, at least he shows me no contempt; whereas the absent man, silently indeed, but very plainly, tells me that he does not think me worth his attention.

—Lord Chesterfield

WE should ever conduct ourselves towards our enemy as if he were one day to be our friend.

—John Henry Newman

NEVER act toward someone as though you were never going to come across him again in life. . . . Never sacrifice what the future may hold for some immediate gain. Be yourself with everyone you meet — but be your best self, for you can be sure that before you have lived out your life you are going to meet again. . . . You always meet people a second time.

—Samuel Goldwyn

WE have learned by sad experience that it is the nature and disposition of almost all men, as soon as they get a little authority, as they suppose, they will immediately begin to exercise unrighteous dominion.

Hence many are called, but few are chosen.

No power or influence can or ought to be maintained . . . only by persuasion, by long-suffering, by gentleness and meekness, and by love unfeigned;

By kindness, and pure knowledge, which shall greatly enlarge the soul without hypocrisy, and without guile—

Reproving betimes with sharpness, . . . and then showing forth afterwards an increase of love toward him whom thou hast reproved, lest he esteem thee to be his enemy.

—Doctrine & Covenants 121:39-43

TWO things, well considered, would prevent many quarrels; first to have it well ascertained whether we are not disputing about terms rather than things; and secondly, to examine whether that on which we differ is worth contending about.

—Charles Caleb Colton

HELP thy brother's boat across, and lo! thine own has reached the shore.

—Hindu Proverb

TO have respect for ourselves guides our morals, and to have a deference for others governs our manners.

—Laurence Sterne

THE greater man, the greater courtesy.

—Alfred Lord Tennyson

KIND words cost no more than unkind ones, . . . and we may scatter the seeds of courtesy and kindliness around us at so little expense. If you would fall into any extreme let it be on the side of gentleness. The human mind is so constructed that it resists vigor and yields to softness.

—Jeremy Bentham

I have no right, by anything I do or say, to demean a human being in his own eyes. What matters is not what I think of him; it is what he thinks of himself. To undermine a man's self-respect is a sin.

—Antoine de Saint-Exupéry

MANNERS are rather to be learnt by example than rules.

—John Locke

AMONG the greatest blessings in life is to be safe with someone — someone without evil intent, someone who wouldn't violate a trust, who wouldn't take advantage of innocence or ignorance; someone who isn't planning in his heart to compromise principles. . . . We may have all else in life, but if we can't count on character, on integrity, if we haven't the sense of being safe, we have little that matters very much.

—Richard L. Evans

BE courteous to all, but intimate with few; and let those few be well tried before you give them your confidence. True friendship is a plant of slow growth, and must undergo and withstand the shocks of adversity before it is entitled to the appellation. Let your heart feel for the affections and distresses of every one, and let your hand give in proportion to your purse; remembering always the estimation of the widow's mite, that it is not every one that asketh that deserveth charity; all, however, are worthy of the inquiry, or the deserving may suffer.

—George Washington

WHEN death, the great reconciler, has come, it is never our tenderness that we repent of, but our severity.

—George Eliot

IF we chance to fix our thoughts
elsewhere,
Though our eyes open be, we cannot
see.

—Sir John Davies

A smile is the light in the window of your face that tells people that your heart is at home.

—Author Unknown

IF we are prudent men, we shall rein in our impulse to affection as we do chariot horses. We make a preliminary trial of horses. So we should of friendship; and should test our friends' characters by a kind of tentative friendship.

—Cicero

ONE of the great discoveries in life is finding a dependable person.

—Richard L. Evans

ON THIS DAY

Mend a quarrel. Search out a forgotten friend. Dismiss suspicion, and replace it with trust. Write a love letter. Share some treasure. Give a soft answer. Encourage youth. Manifest your loyalty in a word or deed.

Keep a promise. Find the time. Forego a grudge. Forgive an enemy. Listen. Apologize if you were wrong. Try to understand. Flout envy. Examine your demands on others. Think first of someone else. Appreciate, be kind, be gentle. Laugh a little more.

Deserve confidence. Take up arms against malice. Decry complacency. Express your gratitude. Worship your God. Gladden the heart of a child. Take pleasure in the beauty and wonder of the earth. Speak your love. Speak it again. Speak it still again. Speak it still once again.

—Author Unknown

WHEN a friend deals with a friend,
Let the bargain be clear and well-
penned,
That they may continue friends to the
end.

—Author Unknown

SHOULD you feel inclined to censure
Faults you may in others view,
Ask your own heart, ere you venture,
If that has not failings too.

Let not friendly vows be broken;
Rather strive a friend to gain;
Many a word in anger spoken
Finds its passage home again.

Do not, then, in idle pleasure,
Trifle with a brother's fame;
Guard it as a valued treasure,
Sacred as your own good name.

Do not form opinions blindly.
Hastiness to trouble tends;
Those of whom we thought unkindly,
Oft become our warmest friends.

—Author Unknown

THE joy of giving to make others happy is one of the fundamental principles of Christianity. He who has not learned this first step in the religion of Christ has not gone very far in the spirit of Him who made the supreme sacrifice for the salvation of man.

—Author Unknown

MORE hearts pine away in secret anguish for unkindness from those who should be their comforters than for any other calamity in life.

—Edward Young

ANYONE can be polite to a king. It takes a gentleman to be polite to a beggar.

—Author Unknown

CEASE to contend one with another; cease to speak evil one of another.

—Doctrine & Covenants 136:23

WITH malice toward none, with charity for all, with firmness in the right, as God gives us to see the right, let us strive on to finish the work we are in; to bind up the nation's wounds; to care for him who shall have borne the battle, and for his widow and for his orphan; to do all which may achieve and cherish a just and lasting peace among ourselves, and with all nations.

—Abraham Lincoln

HE who has one enemy shall meet him everywhere.

—Omar Khayyam

LET us be kind to one another, for most of us are fighting a hard battle.

—Ian Maclaren

WHAT do we live for if it is not to make life less difficult for each other.

—George Eliot

THROW away thy rod,
Throw away thy wrath;
Take the gentle path.

—George Herbert

ALL your strength is in your union.
All your danger is in discord.
Therefore be at peace henceforward,
And as brothers live together.

—Henry Wadsworth Longfellow

Part 13

Principles:
Truth, Beauty,
Love, Virtue,
and
Other Values

Stand with anybody that stands right ... and part with him when he goes wrong.

—ABRAHAM LINCOLN

IF it is not right, do not do it; if it is not true, do not say it.

—Marcus Aurelius

WHY tell me that a man is a fine speaker if it is not the truth that he is speaking?

—Thomas Carlyle

WHEN was public virtue to be found when private was not?

—William Cowper

EVERY man must sometime or other be trusted to himself.

—John Locke

IT is a greater compliment to be trusted than to be loved.

—George Macdonald

NO one can afford to look downward for his enjoyments.

—David Starr Jordan

NEVER give in! Never give in! Never, never, never. Never — in anything great or small, large or petty — never give in except to convictions of honor and good sense.

—Sir Winston Churchill

TO say no at the right time, and then stand by it, is the first element of success. . . . He is the wise man who, for all his life, can keep mind and soul and body clean.

—David Starr Jordan

WITHOUT a moral and spiritual awakening there is no hope for us.

—Dwight D. Eisenhower

THERE is a beauty every girl has — a gift from God, as pure as the sunlight, and as sacred as life. It is a beauty all men love, a virtue that wins all men's souls. That beauty is chastity. A beautiful, modest, chaste woman is creation's masterpiece.

—*David O. McKay*

ONE may be better than his reputation, but never better than his principles.

—*Nicholas V. de Latena*

THE gentleman is a man of truth.

—*Ralph Waldo Emerson*

NOTHING can make a man truly great but being truly good.

—*Matthew Henry*

NO more important duty can be urged upon those who are entering the great theatre of life than simple loyalty to their best convictions.

—*Edwin Hubbel Chapin*

MORALITY . . . alone possesses dignity.

—*Immanuel Kant*

IF any man seeks for greatness, let him forget greatness and ask for truth, and he will find both.

—*Horace Mann*

IN every generation there has to be some fool who will speak the truth as he sees it.

—*Boris Pasternak*

THE most distressing aspect of the world into which you are going is its indifference to the basic issues, which now, as always, are moral issues.

—*Robert M. Hutchins*

THE life of a small group of people, who live true to their convictions, does more and more certain good than all writings. Let us, therefore, young and old, direct all our actions as much as possible towards the realization of our convictions in our life.

—*Tolstoi*

THE earth is the Lord's, and the fulness thereof; the world, and they that dwell therein.

For he hath founded it upon the seas, and established it upon the floods.

Who shall ascend into the hill of the Lord? or who shall stand in his holy place?

He that hath clean hands, and a pure heart; who hath not lifted up his soul unto vanity, nor sworn deceitfully.

He shall receive the blessing from the Lord, and righteousness from the God of his salvation.

—*Old Testament, From Psalm 24*

ONE might well wonder about the term "adult entertainment." Could it be that something unclean or immoral which is not fit for children is wholesome for adults? Is "adult evil" acceptable? How consistent is it to have a double standard?

Or how would anyone be so shortsighted as to partake of that which would impair his physical or mental or spiritual capacity, and say to himself, "It's not good for children, but it's all right for me"?

If a play or entertainment or a movie is crude, low-minded, immoral, should we patronize it?

If the content of a magazine encourages loose morals and low-mindedness and permissive, degrading attitudes and practices, should we buy it? Should we read it? Should we have it around the home?

If a book is filthy, should we buy it? Should we read it? ". . . books," said Thomas Carlyle, "are like men's souls."

—*Richard L. Evans*

TRUTH is the secret of eloquence and of virtue, the basis of moral authority; it is the highest summit of art and life.

—*Henri Frederic Amiel*

HE drew a circle that shut me out—
Heretic, rebel, a thing to flout.
But love and I had the wit to win;
We drew a circle that took him in.

—*Edwin Markham*

VOID of freedom, what would virtue be?

—*Alphonse de Lamartine*

TRUTH often suffers more by the heat of its defenders than from the arguments of its opposers.

—*William Penn*

YOU cannot play with the animal in you without becoming wholly animal, play with falsehood without forfeiting your right to truth, play with cruelty without losing your sensitivity of mind. He who wants to keep his garden tidy doesn't reserve a plot for weeds.

—*Dag Hammerskjold*

IF a man say, I love God, and hateth his brother, he is a liar: for he that loveth not his brother whom he hath seen, how can he love God whom he hath not seen?

—*New Testament, I John 4:20*

MANY people have lost the proper sense of values and have sought the peace and happiness of wealth at the expense of spiritual growth.

—*David O. McKay*

THE pure, the bright, the beautiful
That stirred our hearts in youth,
The impulses to wordless prayer,
The streams of love and truth,
The longing after something lost,
The spirit's yearning cry,
The striving after better hopes—
These things can never die.

The timid hand stretched forth to aid
A brother in his need;
A kindly word in grief's dark hour
That proves a friend indeed;
The plea for mercy softly breathed,
When justice threatens high,
The sorrow of a contrite heart—
These things shall never die.

Let nothing pass, for every hand
Must find some work to do,
Lose not a chance to waken love—
Be firm and just and true.
So shall a light that cannot fade
Beam on thee from on high,
And angel voices say to thee—
"These things shall never die."

—*Charles Dickens*

IT is easy in the world to live after the world's opinions; it is easy in solitude to live after our own; but the great man is he who in the midst of the crowd keeps with perfect sweetness the independence of solitude.

—*Ralph Waldo Emerson*

FOR truth and duty it is ever the fitting time; who waits until circumstances completely favor his undertaking will never accomplish anything.

—*Martin Luther*

SURRENDER your pride to truth.

—*Rabindranath Tagore*

THERE is a comfort in the strength of love:
'Twill make a thing endurable, which else
Would overset the brain, or break the heart.

—*William Wordsworth*

TELL the truth. Live the truth. Live so that you don't have to remember what you said.

—*Richard L. Evans*

ONE truth discovered is a link with the immortal.

—*William Hazlitt*

ALL good things are cheap: all bad are very dear.

—*Henry David Thoreau*

THE world is too much with us; late and soon,
Getting and spending, we lay waste our powers.

—*William Wordsworth*

THE night has a thousand eyes,
And the day but one,
Yet the light of the bright world dies
With the dying sun.

The mind has a thousand eyes,
And the heart but one,
Yet the light of a whole life dies
When its love is done.

—*Francis W. Bourdillon*

SO intimate is the alliance of mind and heart, that . . . the remedy for all blunders, the cure of blindness, the cure of crime, is love; . . . the redeemer and instructor of souls . . . is love.

—*Ralph Waldo Emerson*

IMPORTANT principles may and must be inflexible.

—*Abraham Lincoln*

I have seldom known any one who deserted truth in trifles that could be trusted in matters of importance.

—*William Paley*

LET virtue garnish thy thoughts unceasingly; then shall thy confidence wax strong in the presence of God.

—*Doctrine & Covenants 121:45*

THE principles now implanted in thy bosom will grow, and one day reach maturity; and in that maturity thou wilt find thy heaven or thy hell.

—*David Thomas*

LOVE and you shall be loved.

—*Ralph Waldo Emerson*

ABSENCE is to love what wind is to fire; it extinguishes the small, it enkindles the great.

—*Comte de Bussy-Rabutin*

THERE is no real excellence in all this world which can be separated from right living.

—*David Starr Jordan*

LOVE is lost in immensities; it comes in simple, gentle ways.

—*Joseph Fort Newton*

THE eyes of other people are the eyes that ruin us. If all but myself were blind, I should want neither fine clothes, fine houses, nor fine furniture.

—*Benjamin Franklin*

CONVICTION is worthless unless it is converted into conduct.

—*Thomas Carlyle*

FEW men have virtue to withstand the highest bidder.

—*George Washington*

REMEMBER faith, virtue, knowledge, temperance, patience, brotherly kindness, godliness, charity, humility, diligence.

—*Doctrine & Covenants 4:6*

VIRTUE is the health of the soul.

—*Joseph Joubert*

SINCERE love is something that sacrifices — not something that indulges itself. Sincere love is responsible. It would never knowingly hurt, but would heal.

—*Richard L. Evans*

DEVIATION from either truth or duty is a downward path.

—*Tyron Edwards*

LET me not to the marriage of true minds
Admit impediments. Love is not love
Which alters when it alteration finds,
Or bends with the remover to remove.
O no! it is an ever-fixed mark
That looks on tempests and is never shaken;
It is the star to every wandering bark,
Whose worth's unknown, although his height be taken.
Love's not Time's fool, though rosy lips and cheeks
Within his bending sickle's compass come;
Love alters not with his brief hours and weeks,
But bears it out even to the edge of doom.
    If this be error and upon me proved,
    I never writ, nor no man ever loved.

—Shakespeare, Sonnet cxvi

THE most striking contradiction of our civilization is the fundamental reverence for truth which we profess and the thorough-going disregard for it which we practice.

—Vilhjalmur Stefansson

WHATEVER makes men good Christians, makes them good citizens.

—Daniel Webster

VERACITY does not consist in saying, but in the intention of communicating truth.

—Samuel Taylor Coleridge

HERE we are not afraid to follow the truth wherever it may lead, nor to tolerate any error so long as reason is left free to combat it.

—Thomas Jefferson
(Motto for the U. of Virginia)

AT no age is a man safe in departing from principles.

—Richard L. Evans

ALL truth is safe and nothing else is safe; and he who keeps back the truth, or withholds it from men, from motives of expediency, is either a coward or a criminal, or both.

—Max Müller

LET not sleep fall upon thy eyes till thou has thrice reviewed the transactions of the past day. Where have I turned aside from rectitude? What have I been doing? What have I left undone, which I ought to have done?

—Pythagoras

FACTS do not cease to exist because they are ignored.

—Aldous Huxley

LOVE is not getting, but giving, not a wild dream of pleasure, and madness of desire — . . . it is goodness, and honor, and peace and pure living.

—*Henry Van Dyke*

THOU shalt love thy wife with all thy heart, and shalt cleave unto her and none else.

—*Doctrine & Covenants 42:22*

BLESSED it is to know that neither distance nor death can truly separate those who love.

—*John Muir*

LOVE is a great thing, a good above all others, which alone maketh every burden light. . . . Love is watchful, and whilst sleeping, still keeps watch; though fatigued, it is not weary; though pressed, it is not forced. . . . Love is . . . sincere . . . gentle, strong, patient, faithful, prudent, long-suffering, manly. . . . Love is circumspect, humble, and upright; not weak, not fickle, nor intent on vain things; sober, chaste, steadfast, quiet, and guarded in all the senses.

—*Thomas á Kempis*

THERE are those . . . who tolerate everything because they believe nothing.

—*Robert Browning*

UNLESS virtue guide us our choice must be wrong.

—*William Penn*

THERE are three marks of a superior man: being virtuous, he is free from anxiety; being wise, he is free from perplexity; being brave, he is free from fear.

—*Confucius*

YOUR son was a hero, General;
  Yes sir, I give you my word.
Hundreds of days he was a hero. On
  only one day did he break.
Don't all those other days count for
  anything?

—*Henry Denker and Ralph Berkey*

TRUTH is the most valuable thing we have.

—*Mark Twain*

A gentleman considers what is *right;* the vulgar consider what will *pay.*

—*Confucius*

THIS new morality seems about the same as the old immorality.

—*Author Unknown*

PEOPLE cannot change truth — but truth can change people.

—*Author Unknown*

WE believe in being honest, true, chaste, benevolent, virtuous, and in doing good to all men. . . . If there is anything virtuous, lovely, or of good report or praiseworthy, we seek after these things.

—*Joseph Smith*

NOTHING can be truly great which is not right.

—*Samuel Johnson*

WE have committed the Golden Rule to memory; let us now commit it to life.

—*Edwin Markham*

DO not let us lie at all. Do not think of one falsity as harmless, and another as slight, and another as unintended. Cast them all aside; they may be light and accidental, but . . . it is better that our hearts should be swept clean of them.

—*John Ruskin*

IF you tell the truth you don't have to remember anything.

—*Mark Twain*

NOTHING gives such a blow to friendship as detecting another in an untruth. It strikes at the root of our confidence ever after.

—*William Hazlitt*

HE does not *believe* that does not *live* according to his belief.

—*Thomas Fuller*

THE truth never hurts — unless it ought to.

—*B. C. Forbes*

BEAUTY is the highest expression of morality.

—*Frank Lloyd Wright*

AND ye shall know the truth, and the truth shall make you free.

—*New Testament, John 8:32*

TRUTH is tough. It will not break, like a bubble, at a touch.

—*Oliver Wendell Holmes*

IS not the truth the truth?

—*Shakespeare*

PRINCIPLES don't cease to be principles on Monday morning.

—*Richard L. Evans*

Part 14

Advice, Example, Gossip; Experience and Speaking

There is nothing that can't be made worse by telling.

—TERENCE

YOUR name is safe in our home.

—*Oscar A. Kirkham*

SOMETIMES when I consider what tremendous consequences come from little things . . . I am tempted to think . . . there are no little things.

—*Bruce Barton*

WE give advice by the bucket, but take it by the grain.

—*William R. Alger*

A man cannot speak but he judges himself. With his will, or against his will, he draws his portrait to the eye of his companions by every word. Every opinion reacts on him who utters it.

—*Ralph Waldo Emerson*

SEE that there is . . . neither hardness with each other, neither lying, backbiting, nor evil speaking.

—*Doctrine & Covenants 20:54*

THE foolish and wicked practice of profane cursing and swearing is a vice so mean and low that every person of sense and character detests and despises it.

—*George Washington*

IT is a great misfortune not to have sense enough to speak well, and judgment enough to speak little.

—*Erasmus*

THINK *all* you speak, but speak not *all* you think. Thoughts are your own; your words are so no more.

—*Patrick Delany*

THAT which passes out of one mouth passes into a hundred ears.

—*Ernest Bramah*

WHERE the road bends abruptly, take short steps.

—*Ernest Bramah*

THE true spirit of conversation consists in building on another man's observation, not in overturning it.

—*Edward G. Bulwer-Lytton*

IT is much easier to be critical than to be correct.

—*Benjamin Disraeli*

HE preaches well that lives well, quoth Sancho; that's all the divinity I understand.

—*Cervantes*

MY life is my message.

—*Mahatma Gandhi*

WE have . . . lost the confidence of your children, because of your bad examples before them.

—*Book of Mormon, Jacob 2:35*

A fellow ought to act so that when someone tells his son he reminds him of his father the boy will stick out his chest instead of hanging his head.

—*Author Unknown*

I am a part of all that I have met.

—*Alfred Lord Tennyson*

THE first great gift we can bestow on others is a good example.

—*Sir Charles Morell*

THE best advice for modern people, young and old, facing all sorts of propaganda, is the single word, think.

—*Joseph M. Shaw, Jr.*

THERE would not be so many open mouths, if there were not so many open ears.

—*Joseph Hall*

SHOW me the man you honor, and I will know what kind of a man you are.

—*Thomas Carlyle*

WHEN a man with money meets a man with experience, the man with money gets experience and the man with experience gets the money.

—*William Knudsen*

WHEN will talkers refrain from evil-speaking? When listeners refrain from evil-hearing.

—*August Hare*

ALL the beautiful sentiments in the world weigh less than a single lovely action.

—*James Russell Lowell*

WE often hear people excuse themselves for their uncouth manners and offensive language . . . but we ought to imitate the best speakers, and study to convey our ideas to each other in the best and choicest language. . . . Let not thy tongue give utterance to the evil that is in thine heart, but command thy tongue to be silent until good shall prevail over the evil.

—*Brigham Young*

THE art of being wise is the art of knowing what to overlook.

—*William James*

BLESSED is the man who, having nothing to say, abstains from giving us wordy evidence of the fact.

—*George Eliot*

WHEN you are in company, talk often, but not long; in that case if you do not please, at least you are sure not to tire your listeners.

—*Lord Chesterfield*

ADVICE is seldom welcome. Those who need it most, like it least.

—*Samuel Johnson*

MEND your speech a little, lest it may mar your fortune.

—*Shakespeare*

THE more you can learn from the past, the less you will have to pay for the costly and painful process of trial and error. And deliberately throwing away experience from reliable sources is as foolish, if not more foolish, than deliberately throwing away tangibles.

—*Richard L. Evans*

ONE is thrown in life with a great many people who, though not actively bad, though they may not wilfully lead us astray, yet take no pains with themselves, neglect their own minds, and direct the conversation to petty puerilities or mere gossip, who do not seem to realize that conversation may by a little effort be made instructive and delightful . . . or, on the other hand, may be allowed to drift into a mere morass of muddy thought and weedy words.

—*Sir John Lubbock*

THE path of precept is long, that of example short and effectual.

—*Seneca*

THEY that will not be counselled, cannot be helped. If you do not hear reason she will rap you on the knuckles.

—*Benjamin Franklin*

THE art of conversation is to be prompt without being stubborn, to refute without argument, and to clothe great matters in a motley garb.

—*Benjamin Disraeli*

HARSH counsels have no effect. They are like hammers which are always repulsed by the anvil.

—*Claude Adrien Helvetius*

THE real art of conversation is not only to say the right thing at the right place but to leave unsaid the wrong thing at the tempting moment.

—*Dorothy Nevill*

OUR deeds still travel with us from afar,
And what we have been makes us what we are.

—*George Eliot*

THE best thing to give to your enemy is forgiveness; to an opponent, tolerance; to a friend, your heart; to your child, a good example; to a father, deference; to a mother, conduct that will make her proud of you; to yourself, respect; to all men, charity.

—*Francis Maitland Balfour*

A never failing way to get rid of a fellow is to tell him something for his own good.

—*Frank McKinney Hubbard*

THAT which we are, we are all the while teaching, not voluntarily, but involuntarily.

—*Ralph Waldo Emerson*

LOOK in the face of the person to whom you are speaking if you wish to know his real sentiments, for he can command his words more easily than his countenance.

—*Lord Chesterfield*

ADVICE is not disliked because it is advice, but because so few people know how to give it.

—*Leigh Hunt*

THE trouble with most of us is that we would rather be ruined by praise than saved by criticism.

—*Norman Vincent Peale*

HE who spreads an unreliable rumor shares responsibility with him who starts one.

—*Richard L. Evans*

THE influence of man is not just in what he says, but what he is.

—*Samuel A. Eliot*

ADVICE is like snow; the softer it falls, the longer it dwells upon and the deeper it sinks into, the mind.

—*Samuel Taylor Coleridge*

BEWARE of affectation in speech. It often wrongs matter, and ever shows a blind side.

—*William Penn*

EXPERIENCE keeps a dear school, but fools will learn in no other.

—*Benjamin Franklin*

IF a man thinks he has a superior faith, let him show it by a superior life.

—*Author Unknown*

A gentle, kindly, open communication is one of the essential qualities for the day-to-day understanding of each other and for explaining many moods and avoiding many hurts. There is sometimes need for silence and sometimes need for talk, and both have their place and purpose.

—*Richard L. Evans*

IF any man think it a small matter to bridle his tongue, he is much mistaken.

—*Plutarch*

HAVING lived long, I have experienced many instances of being obliged by better information or fuller consideration to change opinions even on important subjects, which I once thought right, but found to be otherwise.

—*Benjamin Franklin*

BOYS know truth from counterfeit as quick as the chemist does. They detect weakness in your eye and behavior . . . before you open your mouth.

—*Ralph Waldo Emerson*

EDUCATION is what a fellow gets reading the fine print and experience is what he gets by not reading it.

—*Author Unknown*

PROFANITY never did any man the least good. No man is the richer, or happier, or wiser, for it. It commends no one to any society. It is disgusting to the refined; abominable to the good; insulting to those with whom we associate; degrading to the mind; unprofitable, needless, and injurious to society.

—*Author Unknown*

INTO the closed mouth the fly does not get.

—Philippine Proverb

LANGUAGE is the dress of thought; every time you talk your mind is on parade.

—Author Unknown

OF course everything has been said that needs to be said — but since no one was listening it has to be said again.

—Author Unknown

PLEASE, dear God, make my words today sweet and tender, for tomorrow I may have to eat them.

—Author Unknown

WHAT should not be heard by little ears should not be said by big mouths.

—Author Unknown

THERE are words the point of which sting the heart through the course of a whole life.

—Frederika Bremer

THE flying rumors gather'd as they roll'd,
Scarce any tale was sooner heard than told;
And all who told it added something new,
And all who heard it made enlargements too.

—Alexander Pope

THERE'S a lust in man no charm can tame
Of loudly publishing his neighbor's shame;
On eagles' wings immortal scandals fly,
While virtuous actions are but born and die.

—Juvenal

THE true gentleman . . . has his eyes on all his company; he is tender towards the bashful, gentle towards the distant, and merciful towards the absurd; he can recollect to whom he is speaking; he guards against unseasonable allusions, or topics which may irritate; he is seldom prominent in conversation, and never wearisome.

—John Henry Newman

Part 15

Temptation, Repentance; Forgiving and Forgetting

A man who has committed a mistake and doesn't correct it is committing another mistake.

—Confucius

I believe when we repent there is some erasing going on up there so that when we get there we will be judged as we are, for what we are, and maybe not for what we have been!

—*Matthew Cowley*

MEN are punished by their sins, not for them.

—*Elbert Hubbard*

THE sin they do by two and two they must pay for one by one.

—*Rudyard Kipling*

THE only safe ground is so far from danger as it is possible to get.

—*Heber J. Grant*

NO one ever fell over a precipice who never went near one.

—*Richard L. Evans*

OH thou child of many prayers!
Life hath quicksands—life hath snares!

—*Henry Wadsworth Longfellow*

BUT pleasures are like poppies
  spread,
You seize the flow'r, its bloom is shed;
Or like the snow falls in the river,
A moment white — then melts forever.

—*Robert Burns*

TO do it no more is the truest repentance.

—*Martin Luther*

IF you don't want it printed in the paper, don't do it. If you don't want to be quoted, if you don't want it repeated, don't say it. And we might add also: If you don't want it on your conscience, don't do it. If you don't want it in your life, don't do it. We still live in a world of causes and consequences. Our record is with us. If you don't want it printed or repeated or to become part of your record, of your life, don't do it, don't say it.

—Richard L. Evans

THE little I have seen of the world teaches me to look upon the errors of others in sorrow, not in anger. When I take the history of one poor heart that has sinned and suffered, and think of the struggles and temptations it has passed through, the brief pulsations of joy, the feverish inquietude of hope and fear, the pressure of want, the desertion of friends, I would fain leave the erring soul of my fellow-man with Him from whose hands it came.

—Henry Wadsworth Longfellow

AND again, believe that ye must repent of your sins and forsake them, and humble yourselves before God; and ask in sincerity of heart that he would forgive you; and now, if you believe all these things see that ye do them. . . . And behold, I say unto you that if ye do this ye shall always rejoice, and be filled with the love of God, always retain a remission of your sins; and ye shall grow in the knowledge of the glory of him that created you.

*—Book of Mormon, King
Benjamin; Mosiah 4:10, 12*

YOU who are letting miserable misunderstandings run on from year to year, meaning to clear them up some day; you who are keeping wretched quarrels alive because you cannot quite make up your mind that now is the day to sacrifice your pride and [settle] them: You who are passing men sullenly upon the street, not speaking to them out of some silly spite; you who are letting . . . [someone's] heart ache for a word of appreciation or sympathy, which you mean to give him someday; If you only could know and see and feel, all of a sudden, *the time is short,* how it would break the spell! How you would go instantly and do the thing which you might never have another chance to do.

—Phillips Brooks

HE that cannot forgive others breaks the bridge over which he himself must pass if he would ever reach heaven; for every one has need to be forgiven.

—*George Herbert*

A forgiveness ought to be like a cancelled note, torn in two and burned up, so that it never can be shown against the man.

—*Henry Ward Beecher*

SIN with the multitude, and your responsibility and guilt are as great and as truly personal as if you alone had done the wrong.

—*Tryon Edwards*

THERE is much bitterness and blame in deliberately doing something bad — in the headlong, downhill misdoing that goes nowhere to nothing that anyone in his right mind would ever really want. And well would we pause to ask ourselves honestly — always — what would we wish we had done — or hadn't done — tomorrow morning?

—*Richard L. Evans*

SIN is not hurtful because it is forbidden, but it is forbidden because it is hurtful.

—*Benjamin Franklin*

MEN'S hearts ought not to be set against one another, but against evil only.

—*Thomas Carlyle*

EVERY man should have a good-sized cemetery in which to bury the faults of his friends.

—*Henry Ward Beecher*

I, the Lord will forgive whom I will forgive, but of you it is required to forgive all men.

—*Doctrine & Covenants 64:10*

MAN doesn't need to be led into temptation; he usually can find his own way.

—*Brigham Young*

WHEN you make a mistake, don't look back at it long. Take the reason of the thing into your mind, and then look forward. Mistakes are lessons of wisdom. The past cannot be changed. The future is yet in your power.

—*Hugh White*

VICE is a monster of so frightful mien,
As to be hated needs but to be seen;
Yet seen too oft, familiar with her face,
We first endure, then pity, then embrace.

—*Alexander Pope*

JUST this once is a long step, but just once more is an easier step — and so men often find themselves far down the wrong road.

—*Richard L. Evans*

IT is too late? Ah, nothing is too late! Till the tired heart shall cease to palpitate.

—*Henry Wadsworth Longfellow*

MOST people can forgive, but they never forget what they forgave.

—*Author Unknown*

WHY be defeated twice, once by our mistakes and again by our attitude toward them?

—*Lowell Bennion*

TO be always intending to live a new life, but never to find time to set about it, this is as if a man should put off eating, drinking, and sleeping, from one day and night to another, till he is starved and destroyed.

—*John Tillotson*

BLESSED are the merciful: for they shall obtain mercy.

—*New Testament, Matthew 5:7*

A man is most vulnerable when he shuts himself away from those to whom he should keep closest.

—*Richard L. Evans*

ALL the water in the world won't sink a ship unless it gets inside.

—*Author Unknown*

WHEN people once are in the wrong,
Each line they add is much too long;
Who fastest walks, but walks astray,
Is only furthest from his way.

—*Matthew Prior*

ONE of the greatest messages of life is that people *can* repent, *can* improve themselves, *can* improve upon the past.

—*Richard L. Evans*

HE that waits for repentance waits for that which cannot be had as long as it is waited for. It is absurd for a man to wait for that which he himself has to do.

—*William Nevins*

HE who chooses the beginning of a road chooses the place to which it leads.

—*Author Unknown*

LET our thoughts, words, dress and general deportment indicate our belief in the sanctity of the body as the temple of God, even as Paul declared it to be: "Wherefore come out from among [the world] . . . and touch not the unclean thing; and I will receive you, and will be a Father unto you, and ye shall be my sons and daughters." (2 Corinthians 6:17, 18.)

—*Hugh B. Brown*

IMMORALITY in any society is defined by the magnitude of the gap between ideals and behavior.

—*George R. Means*

WHEREFORE, I say unto you, that ye ought to forgive one another; for he that forgiveth not his brother his trespasses standeth condemned before the Lord; for there remaineth in him the greater sin.

—*Doctrine & Covenants 64:9*

REPENTANCE may begin instantly, but reformation often requires a sphere of years.

—*Henry Ward Beecher*

HE that repents is angry with himself; I need not be angry with him.

—*Benjamin Whichcote*

IF you don't want temptation to follow you, don't act as if you are interested.

—*Richard L. Evans*

THE faults of our brothers we should write upon the sands. Their virtues we should write on tablets of love and memory.

—*Author Unknown*

NO man ever became extremely wicked all at once.

—*Juvenal*

RIGHTEOUSNESS exalteth a nation: but sin is a reproach to any people.

—*Old Testament, Proverbs 14:34*

JUST because we may have taken one step down a wrong road is no reason why we have to take two.

—*Richard L. Evans*

WHEN some folks flee from temptation, they leave a forwarding address.

—*Author Unknown*

WE have no right to go near temptation, or in fact to do or say a thing that we cannot honestly ask the blessing of the Lord upon, neither to visit any place where we would be ashamed to take our sister or sweetheart.

The Good Spirit will not go with us on the Devil's ground, and if we are standing alone upon the ground belonging to the adversary of men's souls, he may have the power to trip us up and destroy us. . . . Virtue is more valuable than life. Never allow yourself to go out of curiosity to see any of the "undercrust" in this world. We can't handle dirty things and keep our hands clean.

—*Heber J. Grant*

EVERY smallest stroke of virtue or of vice leaves its ever so little scar.

—*William James*

THEY who engage in iniquitous designs miserably deceive themselves when they think they will go so far and no farther; one fault begets another; one crime renders another necessary; and thus they are impelled continually downward into a depth of guilt, which at the commencement of their career they would have died rather than have incurred.

—*Robert Southey*

THIS is the bitterest of all, to wear the yoke of our wrongdoing.

—*George Eliot*

SOME often repent, yet never reform; they resemble a man travelling in a dangerous path, who frequently starts and stops, but never turns back.

—*Bonnell Thornton*

NO one can ask honestly or hopefully to be delivered from temptation unless he has himself honestly and firmly determined to do the best he can to keep out of it.

—*John Ruskin*

IN the very depths of your soul, dig a grave; let it be as some forgotten spot to which no path leads; and there in the eternal silence bury the wrong which you have suffered. Your heart will feel as if a load had fallen from it, and a divine peace come to abide with you.

—*Author Unknown*

FOR first cometh to the mind the simple suggestion, then the strong imagination, afterwards pleasure, evil affection, assent. And so little by little the enemy entereth in altogether, because he was not resisted at the beginning.

—*Thomas á Kempis*

FOR wide is the gate, and broad is the way, that leadeth to destruction.

—*New Testament, Matthew 7:13*

THERE are a thousand hacking at the branches of evil to one who is striking at the root.

—*Henry David Thoreau*

MEN will be punished for their own sins, and not for Adam's transgression.

—*Joseph Smith*

WHEN a fellow shuts his eyes to temptation he ought to be sure he isn't winking.

—*Author Unknown*

AS long as one lives he will have need of repentance.

—*Samuel Johnson*

THE motive of most forms of sin is the desire to make a short cut to happiness. Temptation promises pleasure without the effort of earning it.

—*David Starr Jordan*

IF we live one way we get one result — if we live another way we get another result. We ought to be smart enough, realistic enough, observant and alert enough to know this, forward as well as backwards.

—*Richard L. Evans*

TO be what we are, and to become what we are capable of becoming, is the only end of life.

—*Robert Louis Stevenson*

HE who has no mind to trade with the devil should be so wise as to keep away from his shop.

—*Robert South*

EVERY temptation that is resisted, every noble aspiration that is encouraged, every sinful thought that is repressed, every bitter word that is withheld, adds its impetus to that great movement which flows towards a richer life and higher character.

—*John Fiske*

THE first step, my son, which one makes in the world, is the one on which depends the rest of our days.

—*Voltaire*

YOU need a change of soul rather than a change of climate.

—*Seneca*

THE world looks like a multiplication-table or a mathematical equation, which, turn it how you will, balances itself. . . . You cannot do wrong without suffering wrong. . . . A man cannot speak but he judges himself. . . . Every secret is told, every wrong redressed, in silence and certainty. . . . The thief steals from himself. The swindler swindles himself. . . . Men suffer all their life long, under the foolish superstition that they can be cheated. But it is . . . impossible for a man to be cheated by anyone but himself. . . . What will you have? quoth God; pay for it and take it. . . . Thou shalt be paid exactly for what thou hast done, no more, no less.

—*Ralph Waldo Emerson*

OPPORTUNITY may knock only once, but temptation keeps banging for years.

—*Author Unknown*

HE who has repented of his sins, the same is forgiven, and I, the Lord, remember them no more.

—*Doctrine & Covenants 58:42*

FOR behold, this life is the time for men to prepare to meet God; yea, behold the day of this life is the day for men to perform their labors. . . . Therefore, I beseech of you that ye do not procrastinate the day of your repentance.

—*Book of Mormon, Alma 34:32-33*

A thousand ills come in through the open door of unresisted temptation.

—*David Starr Jordan*

BY this ye may know if a man repenteth of his sins — behold, he will confess them and forsake them.

—*Doctrine & Covenants 58:43*

WITH the morning cool repentance came.

—*Sir Walter Scott*

THE reputation of a thousand years may be determined by the conduct of one hour.

—*Japanese Proverb*

IF I were sure God would pardon me, and men would not know my sin, yet I should be ashamed to sin, because of its essential baseness.

—*Plato*

THERE is no magic in moderation that will change a vice into a virtue.

—*Richard L. Evans*

WHEN we go too far, it's seldom in the right direction.

—*Arnold Glasow*

WICKEDNESS never was happiness.

—*Book of Mormon, Alma 41:10*

IF a thing is right, it can be done; if wrong, it can be done without.

—*Author Unknown*

YOU cannot repent too soon, because you do not know how soon it may be too late.

—*Thomas Fuller*

O God! Put back Thy universe and give me yesterday.

—*Henry Arthur Jones*

LET us be patient, tender, wise, forgiving,
In this strange task of living.

—*Martin Armstrong*

Part 16

Character, Conscience, and Self-Control

When I do good I feel good. When I don't do good I don't feel good.

—Abraham Lincoln

THE mind is its own place, and in itself can make a heaven of hell, a hell of heaven.

—John Milton

THE worst punishment of all is that in the court of his own conscience no guilty man is acquitted.

—Juvenal

MANY a time I wish I had held my peace.

—Thomas á Kempis

OVER the times thou hast no power. . . . Solely over one man thou hast quite absolute power. Him redeem and make honest.

—Thomas Carlyle

UNLESS the vessel is clean, whatever you pour into it turns sour.

—Horace

THERE is another man within me that's angry with me.

—Thomas Browne

A good conscience never costs as much as it is worth.

—J. A. Petit-Senn

A man's first care should be to avoid the reproaches of his own heart.

—Joseph Addison

THE voice of conscience is so delicate that it is easy to stifle it; but it is also so clear that it is impossible to mistake it.

—Madame de Stael

I desire so to conduct the affairs of this administration that if at the end . . . I have lost every other friend on earth, I shall at least have one friend left, and that friend shall be down inside of me.

—*Abraham Lincoln*

NO man is free who is not master of himself.

—*Epictetus*

FOR as he thinketh in his heart, so is he.

—*Old Testament, Proverbs 23:7*

TO do what we like is sometimes very treacherous.

—*Dr. Aziz Suryal Atiya*

SELF-RESPECT is the noblest garment with which a man may clothe himself.

—*Samuel Smiles*

I feel within me
A peace above all earthly dignities
A still and quiet conscience.

—*Shakespeare and Fletcher*

NO man can be free until he conquers himself.

—*Thomas O'Shaughnessy*

CONSCIENCE warns us as a friend before it punishes as a judge.

—*Stanislaus Leszczynski*

GOODNESS is richer than greatness. It consists not in the outward things we do, but in the inward thing we are.

—*Edwin Hubbel Chapin*

IT is in trifles, and when he is off his guard, that a man best shows his character.

—*Arthur Schopenhauer*

CHARACTER is a victory, not a gift.

—*Ivor Griffith*

WE are allowed a choice at every turn of the road. . . . The Lord is ever willing to whisper in our ears which way we should turn.

—*Dr. Lindsay R. Curtis*

EACH good man has in himself a quiet place wherein he lives however torn seemingly by the passions of the world. That is his citadel, which must be kept inviolate against assaults. That quiet place must be founded upon a rock and the rock must be a belief, a fervent and passionate belief, in the existence of the ultimate good, and a willingness to put forth his strength against the ultimate evil.

—*Dr. Foster Kennedy*

THAT we have so little faith is not sad, but that we have so little faithfulness.

—Henry David Thoreau

NOT a having and a resting, but a growing and a becoming, is the character of perfection. . . . [For] perfection consists in becoming something rather than in having something, in an inward condition of the mind and spirit, not in an outward set of circumstances.

—Matthew Arnold

A man is already of consequence in the world when it is known that he can be relied on, that when he says he knows a thing, he does know it — that when he says he will do a thing, he can do, and does it.

—Samuel Smiles

A man who lacks reliability is utterly useless.

—Confucius

CONSCIENCE is the voice of the soul.

—Jean-Jacques Rousseau

WITHOUT consistency there is no moral strength.

—John J. Owen

TO be deceived by our enemies or betrayed by our friends is insupportable; yet to be deceived by ourselves is worse.

—La Rochefoucauld

INDIVIDUALITY is the salt of common life. You may have to live in a crowd but you do not have to live like it, nor subsist on its food.

—Henry Van Dyke

BY nothing do men show their character more than by the things they laugh at.

—Johann Wolfgang von Goethe

TO be plain with you, friend, you don't carry in your countenance a letter of recommendation.

—Charles Dickens

CONSCIENCE is a thousand witnesses.

—Richard Taverner

SELF-INDULGENCE tastes good. But remember the price — self-loathing.

—Dr. Frank Crane

IT matters not what men assume to be; or good, or bad, they are but what they are.

—Philip James Bailey

HOW shall I be able to rule over others when I have not full power and command over myself?

—Francois Rabelais

NO man can climb out beyond the limitations of his own character.

—John Morley

EVERY man must some time or other be trusted to himself.

—*John Locke*

THERE is no true liberty nor real joy save in the fear of God with a good conscience.

—*Thomas á Kempis*

TRUST that man in nothing who has not a conscience in everything.

—*Laurence Sterne*

A quiet conscience sleeps in thunder.

—*Thomas Fuller*

A man should never be ashamed to own he has been in the wrong, which is but saying in other words that he is wiser today than he was yesterday.

—*Alexander Pope*

FREEDOM is born of self-discipline. No individual, no nation, can achieve or maintain liberty without self-control. The undisciplined man is a slave to his own weaknesses.

—*Alan Valentine*

DISCRETION is being able to raise your eyebrows instead of your voice.

—*Author Unknown*

CONSCIENCE is a divine voice in the human soul.

—*Francis Bowen*

INDEED, we can always better understand and appreciate a man's real character . . . [not so much] by his public exhibition of himself but by the manner in which he conducts himself towards those who are the most nearly related to him, and by his transaction of the commonplace details of daily duty.

—*Samuel Smiles*

THOU art none the holier if thou art praised, nor the viler if thou art reproached. Thou art what thou art.

—*Thomas á Kempis*

THERE is no defect except from within. There is no really insurmountable barrier save your own inherent weakness of purpose.

—*Ralph Waldo Emerson*

OUR character is but the stamp on our souls of the free choices of good and evil we have made through life.

—*John Cunningham Geikie*

IT is a great evil, as well as a misfortune, to be unable to utter a prompt and decided "No."

—*Charles Simmons*

THE first and best victory is to conquer self; to be conquered by self is, of all things, the most shameful and vile.

—*Plato*

CHARACTER is what you are in the dark.

—*Dwight L. Moody*

CONSENT to nothing but what may be suitable to the dignity and excellency of a rational creature. . . . The great principle and foundation of all virtue and worth is . . . this: that a man is able to deny himself his own desires, cross his own inclinations, . . . tho' the appetite lean the other way.

—*John Locke*

HE who is living without discipline is exposed to grievous ruin. . . . Who hath a harder battle to fight than he who striveth for self-mastery? And this should be our endeavor, even to master self, and thus daily to grow stronger than self and go on unto perfection.

—*Thomas d Kempis*

LEARN to say "No"; it will be of more use to you than to be able to read Latin.

—*Charles Haddon Spurgeon*

EVEN when conscience is not so strenuous, it is bad enough, saying to us: You there with your heritage, your opportunities, your home, your friends, look at yourself, no better than you are!

—*Harry Emerson Fosdick*

A man wrapped up in himself makes a very small package.

—*Author Unknown*

THOUGH we travel the world over to find the beautiful, we must carry it with us or we find it not.

—*Ralph Waldo Emerson*

WHEN you do what you know is shady, in order to gain money or other advantage, . . . you've sold yourself, and that is always a fool's bargain.

—*Dr. Frank Crane*

GREATNESS is not so much a certain size
As a certain quality in human lives.

—*Phillips Brooks*

THE influence of a man is not just in what he says [or does] but what he is. Character is singularly contagious.

—*Samuel Eliot*

DO what is right; let the consequence follow;
Battle for freedom in spirit and might;
And with stout hearts look ye forth till tomorrow;
God will protect you; then do what is right!

—*Author Unknown*

A disciplined conscience is a man's best friend.

—*Austin Phelps*

SHAME arises from the fear of men, conscience from the fear of God.

—*Samuel Johnson*

WHAT a curious phenomenon it is that you can get men to die for the liberty of the world who will not make the little sacrifice that is needed to free themselves from their own individual bondage.

—*Bruce Barton*

ONE of life's greatest paradoxes is that nearly everyone wants to improve his circumstances but hardly anyone wants to improve himself.

—*Milton Sills*

NOT education, but character, is man's greatest need and man's greatest safe-guard.

—*Herbert Spencer*

NO man knows how much he can endure until he must. Strength, patience, and ability increase with necessity.

—*Richard L. Evans*

THERE is nothing from without a man, that entering into him can defile him: but the things which come out of him, those are they that defile the man.

—*New Testament, Mark 7:15*

WE will walk on our own feet; we will work with our own hands; we will speak our own minds.

—*Ralph Waldo Emerson*

HE was straight; you could trust him.

—*Petronius*

TIS greatly wise to talk with our own hearts, and ask them how we stand.

—*Edward Young*

THE disease of an evil conscience is beyond the practice of all the physicians of all the countries in the world. I'm sure that is what is bothering a certain individual, who continues to do and say evil things, then wonders what is wrong with him.

—*Author Unknown*

IT is astonishing how soon the whole conscience begins to unravel, if a single stitch is dropped.

—*Charles Buxton*

GOD has given you one face, and you make yourself another.

—*Shakespeare*

ABSTINENCE is as easy to me as temperance would be difficult.

—*Samuel Johnson*

THE only way to cure a bad conscience is to stop doing what we know we shouldn't do, and start doing what we should do.

—*Richard L. Evans*

IT is a very serious duty, perhaps of all duties the most serious, to look into one's own character and conduct, and accurately read one's own heart.

—*Nathaniel Emmons*

THERE is no witness so terrible, no accuser so powerful, as conscience which dwells within us.

—*Sophocles*

THESE two things, contradictory as they may seem, must go together: manly dependence and manly independence, manly reliance and manly self-reliance.

—*William Wordsworth*

THE noblest contribution anyone can make for the benefit of posterity is that of a good character.

—*Author Unknown*

YET there is a dignity in the human spirit which can become most clearly visible in the moment of defeat and disaster.

—*Bruce Catton*

MOST powerful is he who has himself in his own power.

—*Seneca*

CHARACTER is much easier kept than recovered.

—*Thomas Paine*

CHARACTER must stand behind and back up everything.

—*Josiah Holland*

WE cannot live better than in seeking to become better.

—*Socrates*

THE more weakness, the more falsehood; strength goes straight; every cannon-ball that has in it hollows and holes goes crooked.

—*Jean Paul Richter*

TALENT without character, beauty, money, power, influence, eloquence — anything without character — is a hazard and a cause of concern. Character will always be found the best safeguard of virtue — and of all else that makes life safe and satisfying.

—*Richard L. Evans*

THE two powers which in my opinion constitute a wise man are those of bearing and forbearing.

—*Epictetus*

DO you want to know the man against whom you have most reason to guard yourself? Your looking-glass will give you a very fair likeness of his face.

—*Richard Whately*

REMEMBER that no matter what you think or what you do, there are two who will know — you and your Father in Heaven.

—*Author Unknown*

EVERYONE who moves restlessly from place to place and from pleasure to pleasure must finally face this fact: Here I am with myself on my hands.

—*Richard L. Evans*

HE that loses his conscience has nothing left that is worth keeping.

—*Nicholas Caussen*

SOMETIMES and under some conditions it is possible to escape from many things — from prison walls, from false friends, from bad company, from boring people, from old environments — but never from ourselves. When we lie down at night, we are there with our own thoughts — whether we like them or not. When we wake in the morning, we are still there — whether we like us or not. The most persistent thing in life (and, we have no doubt, in death also) is our own consciousness of ourselves. This being so, there is no more pitiable person than he who is uncomfortable in his own company — no matter where he runs, or how fast, or how far.

—Richard L. Evans

SCHOOL thy feelings, O my
    brother;
Train thy warm impulsive soul;
Do not its emotions smother,
But let wisdom's voice control.

School thy feelings; there is power
In the cool, collected mind;
Passion shatters reason's tower,
Makes the clearest vision blind.

—Charles W. Penrose

A guilty conscience needs no accuser.

—English Proverb

A man reveals his character even in the simplest things he does.

—Jean de La Bruyére

I regard that man as lost who has lost his sense of shame.

Titus Maccius Plautus

O, what a tangled web we weave,
When first we practice to deceive.

—Sir Walter Scott

RETURN with honor.

—Motto: Author Unknown

SOME day, in the years to come, you will be wrestling with the great temptation, or trembling under the great sorrow of your life. But the real struggle is here, now. . . . *Now* it is being decided whether, in the day of your supreme sorrow or temptation, you shall miserably fail or gloriously conquer. Character cannot be made except by a steady, long continued process.

—Phillips Brooks

GUILTINESS will speak
Though tongues were out of use.

—Shakespeare

I pray thee, O God, that I may be beautiful within.

—Socrates

WHAT e'er thou art, act well thy part.

—Scottish Proverb

Part 17

Habits, Humor;
Faults
and Fashions

Every generation laughs at the old fashions, but follows religiously the new.

—HENRY DAVID THOREAU

MEN acquire a particular quality by constantly acting in a particular way.

—*Aristotle*

THERE are those who, perhaps, fear less the being in hell than out of fashion.

—*Benjamin Franklin*

THE custom and fashion of today will be the awkwardness and outrage of tomorrow — so arbitrary are these transient laws.

—*Alexander Dumas*

WE live too much in platoons; we march by sections; we do not live in our individuality enough; we are slaves to fashion in mind and heart.

—*Edwin Hubbel Chapin*

FASHION is what one wears oneself. What is unfashionable is what other people wear.

—*Oscar Wilde*

THE fashion wears out more apparel than the man.

—*Shakespeare*

BE not the first by whom the new are tried,
Nor yet the last to lay the old aside.

—*Alexander Pope*

AS good out of the world as out of the fashion.

—*John Clarke*

HABITS are at first cobwebs, then cables.

—*Spanish Proverb*

PLATO once rebuked a person for engaging in a gambling game. And when the person protested that he had only played for a "trifle," Plato replied: "The habit is not a trifle."

—*Plato*

THE habits of time are the soul's dress for eternity.

—*George B. Cheever*

WE first make our habits, and then our habits make us.

—*John Dryden*

CUSTOM may lead a man into many errors, but it justifies none.

—*Henry Fielding*

CULTIVATE only the habits that you are willing should master you.

—*Elbert Hubbard*

THE chains of habit are generally too small to be felt until they are too strong to be broken.

—*Samuel Johnson*

CHECK the beginning:
Once thou might'st have cured,
But now 'tis past thy skill,
Too long hath it endured.

—*Thomas á Kempis*

AN obstinate man does not hold opinions — they hold him.

—*Samuel Butler*

THE power of little things [to build or to destroy] . . . should be the first lesson in life.

—*Russell H. Conwell*

HABIT is either the best of servants or the worst of masters.

—*Nathaniel Emmons*

THE fool, with all his other faults, has this also: he is always getting ready to live.

—*Epicurus*

I will speak ill of no man, not even in matters of truth; but rather excuse the faults I hear charged upon others, and upon proper occasion speak all the good I know of everybody.

—*Benjamin Franklin*

A tree will not only lie as it falls, but it will fall as it leans.

—*Joseph John Gurney*

THERE is no more miserable human being than one in whom nothing is habitual but indecision. . . . Full half the time of such a man goes to the deciding or regretting of matters which ought to be so ingrained in him as practically not to exist for his consciousness at all.

—*William James*

BETTER keep yourself clean and bright; you are the window through which you must see the world.

—*George Bernard Shaw*

WE sow our thoughts, and we reap our actions;
We sow our actions, and we reap our habits;
We sow our habits, and we reap our characters;
We sow our characters, and we reap our destiny.

—*C. A. Hall*

DO not begin to make any thing customary . . . [that] you would not have continue and increase.

—*John Locke*

NATURE didn't make us perfect, so she did the next best thing— she made us blind to our faults.

—*A. J. Marshall*

FASHION is a tyrant from which nothing frees us. We must suit ourselves to its fantastic tastes. But being compelled to live under its foolish laws, the wise man is never the first to follow, nor the last to keep them.

—*Blaise Pascal*

IT is far better to know our own weaknesses and failings than to point out those of others.

—*Jawaharlal Nehru*

THE best humor is that which contains the most humanity, that which is flavored throughout with tenderness and kindness.

—*William Makepeace Thackeray*

THE great crises of life are often like a bolt out of the blue of a summer day; there is not a moment for preparation. In such crises all that a man has been doing in the way of preparation suddenly bears fruit. He often acts instinctively; he does that which he is in the habit of doing and, because he is in the habit of doing his best and all his instincts prompt him to put forth the best that is in him, he seizes the golden moment and does not discover until afterward that it was golden.

—*Hamilton Mabie*

WHAT progress can there be for a man unconscious of his faults? Such a man has lost the fundamental element of growth, which is the realization that there is something bigger, better, and more desirable than the condition in which he now finds himself. In the soil of self-satisfaction, true growth has poor nourishment. . . . Heaven pity the man who is unconscious of a fault! Pity him also who is ignorant of his ignorance!

—*David O. McKay*

THE manner of jesting ought not to be extravagant or immoderate, but refined and witty. . . . There are, generally speaking, two sorts of jests: the one, coarse, rude, vicious, indecent; the other polite, refined, clever, witty [which], if well timed, is becoming to the most dignified person. The other is unfit for any gentleman.

—Cicero

IT is not well to see everything, to hear everything; let many causes of offence pass by us unnoticed.

—Seneca

E'en as he trod that day to God,
so walked he from his birth,
In simpleness and gentleness and
honor and clean mirth.

Rudyard Kipling

ALWAYS we must distinguish between what is funny and what is merely filthy, and never give the credentials of humor to what is low-minded or immoral.

—Richard L. Evans

AND that sarcastic levity of tongue,
The stinging of a heart the world hath
stung.

—Lord Byron

HABITS change into character.

—Ovid

IN my belief, you cannot deal with the most serious things in the world unless you also understand the most amusing.

—Sir Winston Churchill

BEWARE of jokes . . . [from which] we go away hollow and ashamed.

—Ralph Waldo Emerson

EVERYTHING is funny as long as it is happening to somebody else.

—Will Rogers

WHO, for the poor renown of being
smart,
Would leave a sting within a brother's
heart?

—Edward Young

THERE is a humor that heals, a humor that helps, and a humor that harms and hurts. And one kind of humor that hurts is the humor that brings embarrassing attention to adverse personal attributes and physical features; the humor, for example, that ridicules what people can't help: the "baldy," "fatty," "skinny," "stand-up-shorty" kind of humor that is, at best, unkind, and is, at worst, cruel and crude and cutting.

—Richard L. Evans

IT is one thing to be moved by events. It is another to be mastered by them.

—Ralph W. Sockman

TAKE heed of jesting. Many have been ruined by it. — It is hard to jest, and not sometimes jeer too, which often sinks deeper than we had intended.

—*Thomas Fuller*

THERE is both dignified and undignified humor. There is raucous, loud-mouthed humor, uncouth humor. There is evil, offensive humor. And there is high-minded, delightful humor.

—*Richard L. Evans*

NOTHING is easier than fault-finding; no talent, no self-denial, no brains, no character are required to set up in the grumbling business.

—*Robert West*

WITH the fearful strain that is on me night and day, if I did not laugh I should die.

—*Abraham Lincoln*

THE unpolite, impulsive man will sometimes rather lose his friend than his joke. He may surely be pronounced a very foolish person who secures another's hatred at the price of a moment's gratification. . . . Spite and ill-nature are among the most expensive luxuries of life.

—*Samuel Smiles*

IT is human nature for those who are at odds with their neighbors to try to get even.

—*Brigham Young*

DON'T start what you shouldn't do.

—*Author Unknown*

WOMEN'S styles may change, but their designs remain the same.

—*Author Unknown*

WE don't stumble over mountains. We stumble over small things mostly.

—*Author Unknown*

THERE is nothing that a man can less afford to leave at home than his conscience or his good habits.

—*Richardson Packe*

YOU cannot run away from a weakness. You must sometime fight it out or perish. And if that be so, why not now and where you stand?

—*Robert Louis Stevenson*

FAULTS are thick where love is thin.

—*James Howell*

USUALLY our criticism of others is not because they have faults, but because their faults are different from ours.

—*Roger Eastman*

THE greatest of faults . . . is to be conscious of none.

—*Thomas Carlyle*

NOTHING needs reforming so much as other people's habits.

—*Mark Twain*

WHAT we shall be, we are becoming.

—*Old Proverb*

ET each man learn to know himself;
To gain that knowledge let him labor,
Improve those failings in himself
Which he condemns so in his neighbor.
How lenient our own faults we view,
And conscience's voice adeptly smother,
Yet, oh, how harshly we review
The self-same failings in another!

And if you meet an erring one
Whose deeds are blamable and thoughtless,
Consider, ere you cast the stone,
If you yourself are pure and faultless.
Oh, list to that small voice within,
Whose whisperings oft make men confounded,
And trumpet not another's sin;
You'd blush deep if your own were sounded.

And in self judgment if you find
Your deeds to others' are superior,
To you has Providence been kind,
As you should be to those inferior.
Example sheds a genial ray
Of light which men are apt to borrow,
So first improve yourself today
And then improve your friends tomorrow.

—Author Unknown

Part 18

Debt, Money, and Such Matters

The biggest trouble with a sure thing is the uncertainty.

—AUTHOR UNKNOWN

MY father taught me that a bill is like a crying baby and has to be attended to at once.

—Anne Morrow Lindbergh

HE is rich who owes nothing.

—Hungarian Proverb

POVERTY is hard, but debt is horrible.

—Charles H. Spurgeon

WHEN governments go to the poor house, they take their citizens with them.

—Arnold Glasow

I favor the policy of economy, not because I wish to save money, but because I wish to save people.

—Calvin Coollidge

NEVER spend your money before you have it.

—Thomas Jefferson

DO not accustom yourself to consider debt only as an inconvenience; you will find it a calamity.

—Samuel Johnson

NO man can serve two masters. . . . Ye cannot serve God and mammon.

—New Testament, Matthew 6:24

SEEK not for riches but for wisdom; and, behold, the mysteries of God shall be unfolded unto you, and then shall you be made rich. Behold, he that hath eternal life is rich.

—Doctrine & Covenants 11:7

THERE are two ways of being happy: We may either diminish our wants or augment our means — either will do — the result is the same; and it is for each man to decide for himself, and do that which happens to be the easiest. If you are idle or sick or poor, however hard it may be to diminish your wants, it will be harder to augment your means. If you are active and prosperous or young or in good health, it may be easier for you to augment your means than to diminish your wants. But if you are wise, you will do both at the same time, young or old, rich or poor, sick or well; and if you are very wise you will do both in such a way as to augment the general happiness of society.

—*Benjamin Franklin*

YOU cannot help small men by tearing down big men.
You cannot bring about prosperity by discouraging thrift.
You cannot strengthen the weak by weakening the strong.
You cannot lift the wage earner by pulling down the wage payer.
You cannot help the poor man by destroying the rich.
You cannot keep out of trouble by spending more than your income.
You cannot further the brotherhood of man by inciting class hatred.
You cannot establish security on borrowed money.
You cannot build character and courage by taking away man's initiative and independence.
You cannot help men permanently by doing for them what they could and should do for themselves.

—*Attributed to Abraham Lincoln*

IF the nation is living within its income its credit is good. If in some crisis it lives beyond its income for a year or two it can usually borrow temporarily on reasonable terms. But if, like the spendthrift, it throws discretion to the winds, is willing to make no sacrifice at all in spending, extends its taxing up to the limit of the people's power to pay, and continues to pile up deficits, it is on the road to bankruptcy.

—*Franklin D. Roosevelt*

GETTING into debt, is getting into a tanglesome net.

—*Benjamin Franklin*

ALL the good things of the world are no further good to us than as they are of use, and of all we may heap up we enjoy only as much as we can use, and no more.

—*Daniel Defoe*

THE way to stop financial joy-riding is to arrest the chauffeur, not the automobile.

—*Woodrow Wilson*

ANYBODY can cut prices, but it takes brains to make a better article.

—*Philip D. Armour*

LOANS and debts make worries and frets.

—*W. G. Benham*

IT is easy to make the rich poor, but it is not so easy, we have discovered, to make the poor rich.

Sir Ernest Benn

ALL progress is based upon a universal innate desire on the part of every organism to live beyond its income.

—*Samuel Butler*

GREAT is Bankruptcy: the great bottomless gulf into which all Falsehoods, public and private, do sink, disappearing.

—*Thomas Carlyle*

THE cohesive power of public plunder.

—*Grover Cleveland, paraphrasing Calhoun*

IF you want to earn more than you get, you need to be worth more than you are paid.

—*Author Unknown*

WHEN a dollar stays in your community it is still a dollar. But when it goes first to Washington, it is diluted and trimmed and comes back a mighty small piece of change.

—*Dr. A. C. Sudan*

A world where nothing is had for nothing.

—*Arthur Hugh Clough*

THE choice to serve God, worthily made, does not necessarily preclude a home or sufficient money or income, or the things of this world which bring joy and happiness, but it does require that we must not turn away from God and the teachings of Jesus Christ while in the pursuit of our temporal needs.

—*N. Eldon Tanner*

ALL of us could retire nicely, without financial worries, in our old age, if we could dispose of our experiences for what they cost us.

—*Author Unknown*

WHEN prosperity comes, do not use all of it.

—*Confucius*

YOUR employer is going to pay you just what you're worth to his business, but he doesn't know, in looking at you fresh out of school, whether you are going to be worth anything or not — and your asking him lets him know that you are thinking of yourself rather than of his business. He has to make a profit to stay in business. He can't pay you more than you are worth and stay in business.

—*Tom Crowe*

A man in debt is so far a slave.

—*Ralph Waldo Emerson*

A man can have little influence unless he is sound and solvent.

—*Richard L. Evans*

DON'T apologize for fair profit. Unless we produce more than we consume, there can't be any progress, and people can't be kept employed.

—*Richard L. Evans*

THANKS to your success, you now have something to lose.

—*Dag Hammarskjold*

ONE sure way to make life miserable is to live in a manner that you can't afford.

—*Author Unknown*

THINK what you do when you run in debt: you give to another power over your liberty. . . . It is hard for an empty bag to stand upright.

—*Benjamin Franklin*

UNFORTUNATELY some lawmakers think money and legislation will solve all matters whereas only attitude and respect are basic to all problems.

—*Jim Goodwin*

IT is easier to collect money than to spend it wisely.

—*Luther Hodges*

THERE can be no freedom or beauty about a home life that depends on borrowing and debt.

—*Henrik Ibsen*

I have discovered the philosopher's stone that turns everything into gold: it is, 'Pay as you go.'

—*John Randolph*

A mortgage casts a shadow on the sunniest field.

—*Robert G. Ingersoll*

FOR what shall it profit a man, if he shall gain the whole world, and lose his own soul?

—*New Testament, Mark 8:36*

I place economy among the first and most important virtues, and public debt as the greatest of dangers to be feared. To preserve our independence, we must not let our rulers load us with perpetual debt. We must make our choice between economy and liberty or profusion and servitude.

—*Thomas Jefferson*

TOO many people forget that the supreme duty of every man is to make a life, since almost anyone can make a living.

—*R. Roy Keaton*

EXPENDITURE always rises to meet income.

—*Cyril Northcote Parkinson*

ONE of the soundest rules I try to remember when making forecasts in the field of economics . . . is that whatever is to happen is happening already.

—*Sylvia Porter*

FOR which of you, intending to build a tower, sitteth not down first, and counteth the cost, whether he have sufficient to finish it? Lest haply, after he hath laid the foundation, and is not able to finish it, all that behold it begin to mock him, saying, this man began to build, and was not able to finish.

—*New Testament, Luke 14:28-30*

DO not spend money for that which is of no worth nor your labor for that which cannot satisfy.

—*Book of Mormon, II Nephi 9:51*

FIDELITY is seven-tenths of business success.

—*James Parton*

SECURITY is mortals' chiefest enemy.

—*Shakespeare*

GIVE me the money that has been spent in war, and I will clothe every man, woman and child in an attire of which kings and queens would be proud. I will build a schoolhouse in every valley over the whole earth. I will crown every hillside with a place of worship consecrated to the gospel of peace.

—*Charles Sumner*

DEBTS do not dissolve themselves.

—*Richard L. Evans*

IT'S true that you can't take it with you, but folks ought to remember that how you got it may determine where you go.

—*Author Unknown*

CASTLES in the air are all right until we try to move into them.

—*Author Unknown*

THE reason for high taxes is to keep folks from spending their money foolishly on things they want so the government can spend it foolishly on things other folks want.

—*Author Unknown*

THE love of money is the root of all evil.

—*New Testament, I Timothy 6:10*

YOU who help to employ other people fruitfully, and help families to live, are in a sense heroic.

—*Richard L. Evans*

MONEY honestly made and honestly spent is as nearly the root of all physical comfort as money dishonestly made and dishonestly spent is the root of all evil.

—*Author Unknown*

IT'S good to have money and the things that money can buy, but it's good, too, to check up once in a while and make sure you haven't lost the things that money can't buy.

—*George Horace Lorimer*

OF all that Thou shalt give me I will surely give the tenth unto Thee.

—*Old Testament, Genesis 28:22*

THOU shalt truly tithe all the increase of thy seed, that the field bringeth forth year by year.

—*Old Testament, Deuteronomy 14:22*

WILL a man rob God? Yet ye have robbed me. But ye say, Wherein have we robbed thee? In tithes and offerings.

—*Old Testament, Malachi 3:8*

BRING ye all the tithes into the storehouse, that there may be meat in mine house, and prove me now herewith, saith the Lord of hosts, if I will not open you the windows of heaven, and pour you out a blessing, that there shall not be room enough to receive it.

—*Old Testament, Malachi 3:10*

GIVE alms of thy goods, and never turn thy face from any poor man; and then the face of the Lord shall not be turned away from thee.

—*Apocrypha, Tobit 4:7*

REMEMBER the words of the Lord Jesus, how he said, It is more blessed to give than to receive.

—*New Testament. Acts 20:35*

GIVE what you have. To some one, it may be better than you dare to think.

—*Henry Wadsworth Longfellow*

AND I will say to my soul, soul, thou hast much goods laid up for many years; take thine ease, eat, drink, and be merry. But God said unto him, Thou fool, this night thy soul shall be required of thee; then whose shall those things be?

—*New Testament, Luke 12:19-20*

IF we are running deeply into debt, we shall continue to run deeper into debt — unless we change direction.

—*Richard L. Evans*

MAYBE death and taxes are inevitable, but death doesn't get worse every time Congress meets.

—*Joan I. Welsh*

COULD I climb to the highest place in Athens, I would lift up my voice and proclaim, "Fellow citizens, why do ye turn and scrape every stone to gather wealth and take so little care of your children to whom one day you must relinquish it all?"

—*Socrates*

I dreamed that I was at a child's party, in which every means of entertainment had been provided by a wise and kind host. The children had been set free in the rooms and gardens, with no care whatever but how to pass their afternoon rejoicingly. There was music, all manner of amusing books, a workshop, a table loaded with everything nice to eat, and whatever a child could fancy, but in the midst of all this it struck two or three of the more "practical" children that they would like some of the brass-headed nails that studded the chairs, and so they set to work to pull them out. In a little while all the children, nearly, were spraining their fingers in pulling out brass-headed nails. With all that they could pull out they were not satisfied; and then everybody wanted some of somebody else's. And at last the really "practical" and "sensible" ones declared that nothing was of any real consequence that afternoon except to get plenty of brass-headed nails. . . . And at last they began to fight for nail heads, *even though they knew they would not be allowed to carry so much as one brass knob away with them.* But no! it was "Who has most nails? I must have as many as you before I leave the house or I cannot possibly go home in peace." At last they made so much noise that I awoke and thought to myself, "What a false dream that is of *children.* Children never do such foolish things. Only men do."

—*John Ruskin*

THE land enclosed within the fence
  To me seemed very great.
I passed that way from day to day.
  A man stood by the gate
    Who owned the land.

His hair was gray and he was bent
  By years of heavy toil.
"This land," he said, "was my home-
      stead
  And I improved the soil.
  I own the land."

The years passed by; again I chanced
  To pass along the road.
I saw a face I could not place;
  And yet it plainly showed
    He owned the land.

A son perhaps of him I knew;
  At least I would find out,
Before going on where he had gone;
  Who once was there about,
    And owned the land.

The young man took me to a plot
  Where his body lay at rest
From all his toil, improving soil.
  Oh, surely God knows best
    Who owns the land.

—*Hannah C. Ashby*

Part 19

Some Special Days and Seasons and Subjects

*I see not a step before me as I tread
on another year;
But I've left the Past in God's keeping, — the Future His mercy shall
clear;
And what looks dark in the distance
may brighten as I draw near.*

—MARY GARDINER BRAINARD

WE ring the bells and we raise the strain,
We hang up garlands everywhere,
And bid the tapers twinkle fair,
And feast and frolic — and then we go
Back to the same old lives again.

—*Susan Coolidge*

WE are bound by every rule of justice and equity, to give the New Year credit for being a good one until he proves himself unworthy of the confidence we repose in him.

—*Charles Dickens*

LET every man search his heart and his life and consider . . . how good and gracious God has been.

—Editorial: *The Outlook*

FOR like a child, sent with a fluttering light
To feel his way along a gusty night,
Man walks the world. Again, and yet again,
The lamp shall be by fits of passion slain;
But shall not He who sent him from the door
Relight the lamp once more, and yet once more?

—*Farid Ud-Din Attar*

THE holy spirit of the Spring
Is working silently.

—*George Macdonald*

GOD expects from men that their Easter devotions will in some measure come up to their Easter dress.

—*Robert Smith*

OH! its grief and pain ne'er can come again,
And its care lies buried deep;
But what joy untold doth the New Year hold,
And what hopes within it sleep!

—*George Cooper*

THE wintry day, descending to its close,
Invites all wearied nature to repose,
And shades of night are falling dense and fast
Like sable curtains closing o'er the past.
Pale through the gloom the newly fallen snow
Wraps in a shroud the silent earth below
As though 'twere mercy's hand had spread the pall,
A symbol of forgiveness unto all.

—*Orson F. Whitney*

IF spring came but once in a century, instead of once a year, or burst forth with the sound of an earthquake, and not in silence, what wonder and expectation there would be in all hearts to behold the miraculous change! But now the silent succession suggests nothing but necessity. To most men only the cessation of the miracle would be miraculous, and the perpetual exercise of God's power seems less wonderful than its withdrawal would be.

—*Henry Wadsworth Longfellow*

SO then the year is repeating its old story again. We are come once more, thank God! to its most charming chapter. The violets and the May flowers are as its inscriptions or vignettes. It always makes a pleasant impression on us, when we open again at these pages of the book of life.

—*Johann Wolfgang von Goethe*

IT is a time, not for exultation, but for searching of the conscience, for humility of spirit, for the heartfelt prayer of the whole people for light, for guidance, for strength, for sanity, for that passion for righteousness which consumes all pride, scorn, arrogance, and trust in the things that perish.

—Editorial: *The Outlook*

BE at War with your Vices, at Peace with your Neighbors, and let every New Year find you a better man.

—*Benjamin Franklin*

OF the southwind, sweet and low;
Never yet was a springtime
When the buds forgot to blow.

—*Margaret Elizabeth Sangster*

THERE is a line from Lead Kindly Light that moves us gently to a subject that is to all of us of some concern:

". . . And with the morn those angel faces smile;
Which we have loved long since, and lost awhile!"

It is given to all of us, sometime, to ponder the length of life, the purpose of life — the love of life, the love of loved ones — the loss of loved ones. We come alone; we leave alone. We leave our loved ones — or they leave us. Life moves one way. We can't rerun it. And so with all of us there is deep searching of the soul.

And in this context comes the question of the reality of resurrection, and of all that pertains to everlasting life. As the record reads, the resurrected Christ was in the company of others, ". . . being seen of them forty days, . . ." with one or two to five hundred or more witnesses. We have no reason to quarrel with the witness of the record, nor with the reality of everlasting life.

If a man die, he *shall* rise again. And to you who have lost loved ones, we would witness that He who gave us life here, has given us life also hereafter. "And with the morn those angel faces smile; Which we have loved long since, and lost awhile!" "Believest thou this? . . . Yea, Lord: I believe."

—*Richard L. Evans*

THE little cares that fretted me,
I lost them yesterday
Among the fields above the sea,
Among the winds at play;
Among the lowing of the herds,
The rustling of the trees,
Among the singing of the birds,
The humming of the bees.

The foolish fears of what may happen
I cast them all away
Among the clover-scented grass,
Among the new-mown hay;
Among the husking of the corn
Where drowsy poppies nod,
Where ill thoughts die and good are born,
Out in the fields with God.

—*Elizabeth Barrett Browning*

SPRING will be short, and summer will soon be gone.

—*Author Unknown*

WHEN you drink of the water don't forget the spring from which it flows.

—*Charles Dickens*

I have always thought of Christmastime, apart from the veneration due to its sacred name and origin — if anything belonging to it can be apart from that — as a good time; a kind, forgiving, charitable, pleasing time; the only time I knew of in the calendar of the year when men and women seem by one consent to open their shut-up hearts freely.

—*Chinese Proverb*

I like spring, but it is too young. I like summer, but it is too proud. So I like best of all autumn, because its leaves are a little yellow, its tone mellower, its colors richer, and it is tinged a little with sorrow. . . . Its golden richness speaks not of the innocence of spring, nor of the power of summer, but of the mellowness and kindly wisdom of approaching age. It knows the limitations of life and is content.

—*Lin Yutang*

LET no pleasure tempt thee, no profit allure thee, no ambition corrupt thee, to do anything which thou knowest to be evil; so shalt thou always live jollily; for a good conscience is a continual Christmas.

—*Benjamin Franklin*

THE woods are lovely, dark and deep,
But I have promises to keep,
And miles to go before I sleep,
And miles to go before I sleep.

—*Robert Frost*

THOU that hast given so much to us, give one thing more . . . a grateful heart.

—*George Herbert*

LET never day or night unhallowed pass, But still remember what the Lord hath done.

—*Shakespeare*

I heard the bells on Christmas day
Their old familiar carols play;
And wild and sweet the words repeat
Of peace on earth, good will to men.

I thought how, as the day had come,
The belfries of all Christendom
Had roll'd along th' unbroken song
Of peace on earth, good will to men.
And in despair I bowed my head:
"There is no peace on earth," I said,
"For hate is strong and mocks the song
Of peace on earth, good will to men."

Then pealed the bells more loud and
     deep:
"God is not dead, nor doth he sleep;
The wrong shall fail, the right prevail,
With peace on earth, good will to
     men."

—*Henry Wadsworth Longfellow*

THESE are the gifts I ask of Thee,
     Spirit serene:
Strength for the daily task,
Courage to face the road,
Good cheer to help me bear the traveler's load,
     And, for the hours of rest that come between,
An inward joy of all things heard and seen.

—*Henry Van Dyke*

HELP us rightly to remember the birth of Jesus, that we may share in the song of the angels, the gladness of the shepherds, and the worship of the Wise Men. Close the door of hate and open the door of love all over the world. Let kindness come with every gift, and good desire with every greeting. Deliver us from evil by the blessings that Christ brings, and teach us to be merry with clean hearts. May the Christmas morning make us happy to be Thy children, and the Christmas evening bring us to our beds with grateful thoughts; forgiving and forgiven, for Jesus' sake. Amen.

—Robert Louis Stevenson
"A Christmas Prayer"

OH give us once again the faith of children that we may no more "torture ourselves with disbeliefs," but come at last to know and to acknowledge, from the certainty of our souls, that Jesus is the Christ, the divine Son of God, our Lord and Savior, the Messiah, the Prince of Peace. "God bless us, everyone" and keep within our hearts and homes that which would bring to each of us the precious gift of personal peace. ". . . Except ye . . . become as little children, ye shall not enter into the kingdom of heaven."

—Richard L. Evans

AND he who receiveth all things with thankfulness shall be made glorious; and the things of this earth shall be added unto him.

—Doctrine & Covenants 78:19

THEN shall the King say unto them on his right hand, Come ye blessed of my Father, inherit the kingdom prepared for you from the foundation of the world:

For I was an hungred, and ye gave me meat: I was thirsty, and ye gave me drink: I was a stranger, and ye took me in:

Naked, and ye clothed me: I was sick, and ye visited me: I was in prison, and ye came unto me.

Then shall the righteous answer him, saying, Lord, when saw we thee an hungred, and fed thee? or thirsty, and gave thee drink?

When saw we thee a stranger, and took thee in? or naked, and clothed thee?

Or when saw we thee sick, or in prison, and came unto thee?

And the King shall answer and say unto them, Verily I say unto you, Inasmuch as ye have done it unto one of the least of these my brethren, ye have done it unto me.

—New Testament, Matthew 25:34-40

AT Christmas — the season
    Of giving and sharing,
Of living and loving,
    Remembering, caring —
Our thoughts bridge the space that
    Would tend to divide us,
Restoring the warmth of
    Your presence beside us.
May all the sweet magic
    Of Christmas conspire
To gladden your hearts
    And fill every desire.

—Harold H. Bennett

ONE could not, of course, conceive of Christmas without Him whose coming it commemorates: the Prince of Peace, the Son of God, our Saviour and Redeemer, concerning whom we witness that He lives. Oh, may we not forget at any time what God has given, or overemphasize the troubles of our time, but go with patience, gratitude and faith into the future.

—*Richard L. Evans*

GRATITUDE is the sign of noble souls.

—*Aesop*

I know that my redeemer liveth, and that he shall stand at the latter day upon the earth

—*Old Testament, Job 19:25*

HRE you willing to forget what you have done for other people, and to remember what other people have done for you; to ignore what the world owes you, and to think what you owe to the world; to put your rights in the background, and your duties in the middle distance, and your chances to do a little more than your duty in the foreground; to see that your fellowmen are just as real as you are; and try to look behind their faces to their hearts, hungry for joy; to own that probably the only good reason for your existence is not what you are going to get out of life, but what you are going to give to life; to close your book of complaints against the management of the universe, and look around you for a place where you can sow a few seeds of happiness — are you willing to do these things even for a day? Then you can keep Christmas.

Are you willing to stoop down and consider the needs and the desires of little children; to remember the weakness and loneliness of people who are growing old; to stop asking how much your friends love you, and ask yourself whether you love them enough; to bear in mind the things that other people have to bear on their hearts; to try to understand what those who live in the same house with you really want, without waiting for them to tell you; to trim your lamp so that it will give more light and less smoke, and to carry it in front so that your shadow will fall behind you; to make a grave for your ugly thoughts and a garden for your kindly feelings, with the gate open — are you willing to do these things even for a day? Then you can keep Christmas.

Are you willing to believe that love is the strongest thing in the world — stronger than hate, stronger than evil, stronger than death — and that the blessed life which began in Bethlehem nineteen hundred years ago is the image and brightness of the Eternal Love? Then you can keep Christmas.

And if you keep it for a day, why not always?

But you can never keep it alone.

—*Henry Van Dyke*

Part 20

Some Random Thoughts and Themes

It is easier to keep up than to catch up.

LEO D. BARDSLEY

YOU never get a second chance to make a good first impression.

—*Author Unknown*

THE best tranquilizer is a clear conscience.

—*Author Unknown*

MANY of us expect an unlimited number of second chances.

—*Author Unknown*

YOU can tell the ideals of a nation by its advertisements.

—*Douglas*

TELEVISION has within its power to decide what kind of people we become. Nothing less.

—*Rt. Hon. W. F. Deedes, M.P.*

NOW that the world has the facilities for transmitting intelligence rapidly it is said they are having difficulty finding enough to transmit.

—*Author Unknown*

ONE of the things the news media does very well is to make a minority look like a majority.

—*Author Unknown*

IF you keep your mind sufficiently open, people will throw a lot of rubbish into it.

—*William A. Orton*

YOU may not remember that far back, but once upon a time movies were rated on how good they were, not on who was allowed to see them.

—*Changing Times*

IF we don't change direction, we will arrive at where we are going.

—*Richard L. Evans*

WHAT this world needs right now is someone who can foretell the future and then change it before it happens.

—*Author Unknown*

THE future is something which everyone reaches at the rate of sixty minutes an hour, whatever he does, whoever he is.

—*Clive Staples Lewis*

PROCRASTINATION is the art of keeping up with yesterday.

—*Don Marquis*

WHAT would be the use of immortality to a person who cannot use well a half hour.

—*Ralph Waldo Emerson*

THE world owes you a living only when you have earned it.

—*Author Unknown*

THESE times of ours are serious and full of calamity, but all times are essentially alike.

—*Ralph Waldo Emerson*

AT times the whole world seems to be in conspiracy to importune you with emphatic trifles.

—*Ralph Waldo Emerson*

WE do have a suspicion, that it is nearly impossible for any body to put himself in another's place. Who is this man who asks you to put yourself in his place? . . . The differences are endless. . . .

—*William Feather*

THE brightest things you ever say
Are those you think about next day.

—*Arnold Glasow*

ADVICE to speakers:
If you don't strike oil in twenty minutes stop boring.

—*Adam S. Bennion*

THE easiest way to stay awake during an after dinner speech is to deliver it.

—*Herman Herst, Jr.*

THEY may forget what you said — but they will never forget how you made them feel.

—*Carl W. Buehner*

NEVER make a promise in haste.

—*Mahatma Gandhi*

HOUSEWORK is what women do that nobody notices until they don't. do it.

—*Author Unknown*

CONVERSATION is the art of telling people a little less than they want to know.

—*Franklin P. Jones*

MEN often oppose a thing merely because they have had no agency in planning it, or because it may have been planned by those whom they dislike.

—*Alexander Hamilton*

TO get the whole world out of bed
And washed, and dressed, and
  warmed, and fed,
To work, and back to bed again,
Believe me, Saul, costs worlds of pain.

—*John Masefield*

IF you must tell all you know, make sure that's all.

—*Author Unknown*

MEANINGS are in people . . . not in words . . .

—*Author Unknown*

THE man who says just what he thinks should think.

—*Author Unknown*

THOUGHTS, from the tongue that slowly part,
Glance quick as lightning through the heart.

—*Sir Walter Scott*

ANYTHING worth saying has already frequently been said. Anything hitherto unsaid should be regarded with the greatest suspicion.

—*Sir Eric Ashby*

A very great part of the mischiefs that vex this world arise from words.

—*Edmund Burke*

WHAT a good thing Adam had — when he said a good thing, he knew nobody had said it before.

—*Mark Twain*

HOW long halt ye between two opinions?

—*Old Testament, I Kings 18:21*

THERE are no successful sinners. All must one day stand before God and be judged.

—*Harold B. Lee*

THE way to change is to change. The way to repent is to depart from former practices.

—*Richard L. Evans*

TEACH me to feel another's woe,
To hide the fault I see;
That mercy I to others show,
That mercy shown to me.

—*Alexander Pope*

THERE is no dishonor in rethinking a problem.

—*The Royal Bank of Canada
Monthly Letter*

I beseech you . . . , think it possible that you may be mistaken.

—*Oliver Cromwell*

A person's ability to forgive is in proportion to the greatness of his soul. Little men cannot forgive.

—*Author Unknown*

RESTLESSNESS is discontent, and discontent is the first necessity of progress.

—*Thomas A. Edison*

THE first faults are theirs that commit them; The second faults theirs that permit them.

—*Thomas Fuller*

WE have been so anxious to give our children what we didn't have that we have neglected to give them what we did have.

—*Author Unknown*

I wonder if ever you change human beings with arguments alone: either by peppering them with little sharp facts or by blowing them up with great guns of truth. You scare 'em, but do you change 'em?

—*David Grayson*

THERE are some who would rather lose a friend than lose an argument — or so it seems.

—*Richard L. Evans*

IT'S pretty hard to tell what does bring happiness. Poverty an' wealth have both failed.

—*Kin Hubbard*

FIVE minutes of today are worth as much to me as five minutes in the next millenium.

—*Ralph Waldo Emerson*

YOUR destiny is in your hands, and your important decisions are your own to make.

—*Spencer K. Kimball*

IF, of all sad words of tongue or pen,
The saddest are, "It might have been,"
More sad are these we daily see,
"It is, but it hadn't ought to be."

—*Bret Harte*

YOU cannot do wrong and feel right.

—*Ezra Taft Benson*

PARENTS can tell, but never teach,
Unless they practice what they preach.

—*Arnold Glasow*

HE who sleeps in continual noise is wakened by silence.

—*W. D. Howells*

I can make a lord, but only the Almighty can make a gentleman.

—*King James I*

NOR can he reasonably expect the confidence of others who too apparently distrusts himself.

—*Samuel Johnson*

TO cure is the voice of the past; to prevent, the divine whisper of today.

—*John Harvey Kellogg*

NO snowflake in an avalanche ever feels responsible.

—*Stanislaus Leszczynski*

EACH of us is part of the problem or part of the answer.

—*Author Unknown*

ONE must separate from anything that forces one to repeat "No" again and again.

—*Friedrich Nietzsche*

THERE are times when if you are not feeling like yourself, it is quite an improvement.

—*Author Unknown*

THOSE who have been given a little authority begin to think what they could do with a little more authority.

—*Richard L. Evans*

THERE is no such thing in human existence as being so high you're not responsible to anybody.

—*Lawrence A. Appley*

IT'S a wise father who throws away his old report cards.

—*Author Unknown*

HE gives twice who gives quickly.

—*Old Proverb*

MY mind is a chest of drawers. When I wish to deal with a subject, I shut all the drawers but the one in which the subject is to be found. When I am wearied, I shut all the drawers and go to sleep.

—*Napoleon Bonaparte*

ONE moment of a man's life is a fact so stupendous as to take the lustre out of all fiction.

—*Ralph Waldo Emerson*

WHEN everybody thinks alike, nobody thinks very much.

—*Author Unknown*

MEN are like children and children are like spaghetti. You can pull them but you can't push them.

—*Author Unknown*

THE best leaders train leaders while they are leading.

—*Author Unknown*

THE only way to do anything is the way it ought to be done.

—*Author Unknown*

IF you draw your thread too fine it will break.

—*Petrarca*

THERE is something more powerful than anybody — and that is everybody.

—*Captain Eddy Rickenbacker*

GOD bless all little boys who look like Puck,
    With wide eyes, wider mouths and stick-out ears,
Rash little boys who stay alive by luck
    And Heaven's favor in this world of tears.

—Arthur Guiterman

WHEN school grades are not] so good as [a father] thinks they should be, he scolds his son . . . though he knows it's the teacher's fault. . . . Fathers grow old faster than people. . . . [Fathers can't cry] while mothers can cry where it shows. . . . Fathers are what give daughters away to other men who are not nearly good enough . . . so they can have grandchildren that are smarter than anybody's.

—Paul Harvey

MORE than one splendid idea has been launched to accomplish a great good only to wind up as an institution more interested in maintaining its routine of procedure rather than in spreading its splendid idea.

—Chesley R. Perry

IF I am not happy with me, other people suffer.

—Neal A. Maxwell

I may be losing my eyesight, but not my vision.

—James C. Penney

THERE are so many labor-saving devices on the market today that a man has to work all his life to pay for them.

—A. J. Marhall

A philosopher is a man who doesn't know either but he's willing to put it into words that will keep you guessing.

—Author Unknown

I hold it to be a fact, that if all persons knew what each said of the other, there would not be four friends in the world.

—Blaise Pascal

IF you want to test your memory, try to recall what you were worrying about one year ago today.

—Rotarian

I think there is only one quality worse than hardness of heart, and that is softness of head.

—Theodore Roosevelt

WHAT is true by lamplight is not always true by sunlight.

—Joseph Joubert

WHEN a man has not a good reason for doing a thing, he has one good reason for letting it alone.

—Thomas Scott

THE things most people want to know about are usually none of their business.

—George Bernard Shaw

I read in a book that a man called Christ went about doing good. It is most disconcerting to me to find that I am so easily content with just going about.

—Toyohiko Kagawa

THE road to ruin is always in good repair; the travellers pay the expense of it.

—W. G. Benham

A cynic is a man who knows the price of everything and the value of nothing.

—Oscar Wilde

LET men decide firmly what they will not do, and they will be free to do vigorously what they ought to do.

—Mencius

THOSE who cannot remember the past are condemned to repeat it.

—George Santayana

LET every man sing his own song in life.

—John A. Widtsoe

THERE is no institution so pure and excellent which the corruption and folly of man will not in time alter for the worse, and load with additions foreign to its nature and original design.

—Johann Lorenz Von Mosheim

PEOPLE must be changed . . . goodness cannot be legislated.

—Spencer W. Kimball

EVERY time history repeats itself it does so at a higher price.

—Author Unknown

PSYCHIATRISTS say talking helps solve problems — Causes 'em too.

—Arnold Glasow

WHEN a fellow begins to understand that he doesn't understand, he's beginning to understand.

—Author Unknown

A fanatic is one who increases his speed after he loses his way.

—Craft M. Pentz

NEVER point a gun at anything you don't intend to shoot.

—Author Unknown—

ALL Indians walk single file — at least the one I saw did.

—An Old Saying

WE aim above the mark to hit the mark.

—*Ralph Waldo Emerson*

IF you think you have a solution, you must not have understood the problem.

—*Author Unknown*

THE hardest trial of the heart is, whether it can bear a rival's failure without triumph.

—*Aikin*

HE who stops being better stops being good.

—*Oliver Cromwell*

HISTORIANS have done the most to change the course of history.

—*Author Unknown*

WE must never become so busy slapping at mosquitoes that we walk into the quicksand.

—*Richard L. Evans*

THE greatest waste in the world is the difference between what we are and what we could be.

—*John Grimes*

WHERE shall I begin, please your Majesty?" he asked. "Begin at the beginning," the King said, very gravely, "and go on till you come to the end: then stop."

—*Lewis Carroll*

DON'T ever take a fence down until you know the reason why it was put up.

—*Gilbert Keith Chesterton*

ALWAYS take a job that's too big for you, and then do your best.

—*Harry Emerson Fosdick*

EVERY man complains of his memory but no man complains of his judgment.

—*Author Unknown*

IF the world learned from history, how different both would be.

—*Arnold Glasow*

EVERY war is a national calamity whether victorious or not.

—*Gen. Von Moltke*

THE song I came to sing remains unsung. I have spent my life stringing and unstringing my instrument.

—*Rabindranath Tagore*

COME, my friends,
'Tis not too late to seek a newer world.

—*Alfred Lord Tennyson*

WE have nothing to lose — except everything.

—*Albert Camus*

MY husband never forgets an anniversary — because I won't let him.

—*Sara M. Tanner*

MY soul, sit thou a patient looker-on;
Judge not the play before the play is done:
Her plot hath many changes; every day
Speaks a new scene; the last act crowns the play.

—Francis Quarles

WE are most of us very lonely in this world; you who have any who love you, cling to them and thank God.

—Author Unknown

DON'T try to live too many days at a time.

—Harold B. Lee

DO you want to repent or rationalize?

—Hugh B. Brown

I shall be telling this with a sigh
Somewhere ages and ages hence:
Two roads diverged in a wood, and I—
I took the one less traveled by
And that has made all the difference.

Robert Frost

GOOD men have the fewest fears.

—Christian Nestell Bovee

IT will take,
I think,
A long time
To learn how.

Should we not
Start now?

—Carol Lynn Pearson

THE past is to learn from and not to live in.

—Richard L. Evans

SUCCESS is never final.

—Author Unknown

Index to Authors